THE POETRY OF ROCK

"WIGGY WORDS THAT FEED YOUR MIND."
—Life Magazine

"**The Poetry of Rock** is not only what's happening but it is an enormously powerful singing collection . . . And it could be the morning star of a renaissance in poetry. I expect that people will be reading it for a long time as an important document in English letters. Those who haven't heard these lyrics or read these poems may deem such a remark extravagant. I feel sorry for them. In this instance the kids with an intuition which is at the base of response to all good poetry, dig more than the critics!"
—Robert R. Kirsch, Book Editor,
Los Angeles Times

Richard Goldstein's comments, put-downs and cogent analyses of the past, present and future of rock appear regularly in "The Village Voice," "The New York Times," "Vogue" and "New York Magazine." Mr. Goldstein lives in New York with his wife and Woodlawn-Jerome, their best friend.

THE POETRY OF ROCK

EDITED BY
RICHARD GOLDSTEIN

THE POETRY OF ROCK

A Bantam Book / February 1969

2nd printing .... May 1969	7th printing ..... June 1972
3rd printing .... August 1969	8th printing .. January 1973
4th printing .... January 1970	9th printing ... October 1973
5th printing ...... June 1970	10th printing ... October 1974
6th printing .... May 1971	11th printing ...... July 1975
	12th printing ..... August 1976

ISBN 0-553-10332-6

Published simultaneously in the United States and Canada

For my brother, Pret.

CONTENTS

Homburg   Keith Reid
Dress Rehearsal Rag   Leonard Cohen
A Day in the Life   Lennon & McCartney
Subterranean Homesick Blues   Bob Dylan
Crucifixion   Phil Ochs
New York Mining Disaster—1941   Barry & Robin Gibb
The Sound of Silence   Paul Simon
Horse Latitudes   The Doors
The End   The Doors

Acknowledgments

I want to acknowledge the assistance of Mr. Russel Sanjek, Vice President for Public Relations at Broadcast Music, Inc. (BMI) and a true connoisseur of rock music. Without his help this book could never have been brought together in its present form. I also want to thank Mrs. Harriet B. Gilmour and Miss Nancy Milner for their work in preparing this book for publication. Finally, I want to thank my wife, Judith, who was called upon to edit, research copyrights, and sing falsetto parts on especially tricky numbers.

Preface

A proper preface tells you how and why a book was written, and who helped put it together. This book was produced by a simple, if tiresome, process of elimination. I examined the catalogues of ASCAP and BMI through the "rock years" (1952 to 1968). I selected and obtained accurate lead sheets for a great many songs. But in transposing these lyrics into verse, I discovered that mere linearity can destroy a rock lyric. In print, robbed of all tonality, a full third of my songs were reduced to drivel. I remembered a bit on the old Steve Allen Show, in which pop lyrics were read aloud in a pseudo-poetic setting. I recall being pretty pissed off with Steverino then for his dishonest presentation of rock. Of all the arguments lodged against rock during its youth, the one that struck me as having the least validity was the charge that pop lyrics were illiterate. Of course they were; that was their greatest virtue.

If any volume of major contemporary poetry were set to music and sounded ridiculous, would we blame the poet for his failure to anticipate this contingency? Or would we reason that his words should not be expected to shine in partnership with rhythm and melody? Well, the reverse is also true. Rock was meant to be heard, not seen. In a sense, this book violates a timeless pop taboo; it imposes one form upon another. In penitence, I admit that all rock lyrics are altered by versification. But not all suffer castration as well. Often, the power and energy in these songs survives transformation. I have tried to facilitate this survival by moving repetitious choruses to the end of songs and excluding identical verses when they appear many times. In some cases—when I felt that such repetition created a trance-like effect which was essential to the lyric—I left the entire song intact. Most of the lyrics which appear here remain exactly as they were on record.

I want to make it clear that this is not a collection of great rock songs. It is meant to function as a representative cross-section of lyrics, illustrating some of rock's distinctive strengths and weaknesses. Many songs which I wanted to include were unavailable for publication here. Others, as I mentioned before, could not be reproduced in verse without being demolished.

I do not claim that these selections constitute a body of "undiscovered" poetry. This is no pop-Ossian. But I do assert that there is an immense reservoir of power here, an impressive awareness of language, and a profound sense of rhythm. I call those qualities "poetic"; you may want to call them "unconscious," but I do not see how the two are incompatible.

At any rate, I suggest that you read these lyrics with their context in mind. This may mean suspending some of your fondest expectations of poetry. Don't expect a rock lyric to move like a poem. You may be used to a loose or even non-existent meter in verse, but rhythm in rock is a matter of propulsion. Awkwardness (and some of these songs are terribly ungainly) is unforgivable in serious verse but can be charming in rock. Finally, rock cultivates cliches. Pop lyricists cherish their involvement with the mundane. This embrace of the pedestrian makes it difficult for the "adult" within us to accept rock as an artform-without-portfolio. We like our culture classy. But it is my opinion—and one on which I base all my writing and this book—that mass culture can be as vital as high art.

America's single greatest contribution to the world has been her Pop (music, cinema, painting, even merchandising). It is with this sense of America, as clown-guru to the world, that I offer the premise of rock poetry. I am aware that certain aspects of pop walk a delicate line between camp and revelation. But I set out to edit this book as a participant, not an authority. So, I welcome your derision—and your heads.

Introduction

Ten years ago, a single, all-embracing criterion governed the evaluation of a rock song. When matters of taste were at hand, you simply arched your back against the nearest lamppost, fixed the buckle of your garrison belt across your hip, and drawled with a hint of spittle between your teeth: "I like it. It's got a good beat. Y'can dance to it."

But those days of aesthetic simplicity have vanished with cinch belts and saddle shoes. Today's rock partisan—plugged into a stereophonic nirvana—is more likely to arch his eyebrows than his pelvis. He may casually remark, with a gleam in his hookah, "I empathize with it. It has truth and beauty. Besides, my kids say it's psychedelic."

Rock 'n' roll has come a long way from its origins in the bargain basement of American culture. Once a pariah of the musical world, it has evolved into a fullfledged artform, perhaps the most preened and pampered of our time. Critics gush superlatives over the Beatles in little magazines. Bob Dylan addresses poets from the far side of Desolation Row, muttering nursery rhymes that fall like a well-oiled guillotine across their necks. Jazzmen do their thing in hippy beads. Serious composers marvel at the Beach Boys while filmmakers search for alienation behind the Doors.

Rock is de rigueur. Hip Broadway turns the Hadassah on, while psychedelic swamis sell aspirin on tv. San Francisco is a teenybopper's holy land; London, a plastic Lourdes. Even Plato's Cave has become a discotheque. Amid its electronic shadows, longhaired princes tell it like it is. So shove over, Norman Mailer, Edward Albee, Allen

1

Ginsberg, and Robert Lowell—make room for the Electric Prunes.

> I've got no kick against modern jazz,
> Unless they try to play it too darn fast;
> And change the beauty of the melody,
> Until they sound just like a symphony,
> That's why I go for that rock 'n' roll music
> Any old way you choose it;
> It's got a back beat, you can't lose it,
> Any old time you use it.
> It's gotta be rock 'n' roll music
> If you wanna dance with me.*

So wrote Chuck Berry, America's first rock poet, in 1957. When he burst upon the scene, with his hips as smooth as gears and his suit spangled with delight, pop music was sharply divided along racial lines, as it had been in America since before the invention of the phonograph. The black sound of the Fifties was Rhythm and Blues, a blunt, joyous party-jive with its language rooted in funky jazz. White America first received this message from black performers like Little Richard, Fats Domino, and Chuck Berry.

But Chuck Berry was special. He sang about an America of pure motion and energy. While the beats did battle with materialism in search of pure spirit, he spent his time behind the wheel of a new Ford, digging speed. Words and images spilled in stacatto freeform across the body of his songs. He chose to work in bold clean shapes, rendered heroic by their sheer simplicity. In a Chuck Berry song, you couldn't tell the girls from the cars, and some of the best marriages ended up in traffic court. He could be as dazzling as a comet or as sentimental as a greeting card. But he was always wry, even in anger. His protest songs made you feel good instead of grim.

Only when he wrote about his music did Chuck Berry get serious. He virtually defined rock for the generation to come as the sound of an inner volcano, the hum of satisfied machinery, the triumph of the material not over, but in conjunction with, the soul.

Today, his lyrics have been largely ignored in the search

for conscious poetry which dominates the rock scene. But behind the bouncing pop ball we seem so eager to follow lies a tradition rich in the kind of accidental art that Chuck Berry provided. No wonder auslanders like the Beatles began their careers in conscious imitation. In Chuck Berry's reckless comic energy they found a vision of America.

At its core, good rock has always provided that kind of mystical experience. But few adults tried to penetrate its gaudy cliches and rigid structure—until now. Today, it is possible to suggest without risking defenestration that some of the best poetry of our time may well be contained within those slurred couplets. But even its staunchest adult partisans seem to think that rock sprang fullblown from the electric loins of the Sixties. The Beatles get some credit for turning a primitive form into art; or, as one respected straight critic put it, for carrying pop music "beyond patronization." But beneath its sequined surface rock has always contained a searing power to communicate where being young and yearning was at. Like blues, it became respectable only after its period of greatest vitality had passed.

> Gonna tell Aunt Mary
> 'Bout Uncle John,
> He says he has the blues
> But he has a lot of fun.
>
> Oh baby,
> Yes baby,
> Woo, baby,
> Havin' me some fun tonight.*

Contemporary rock (sometimes known in post-graduate circles as the "new music") is a mulatto. It was born of an unholy alliance between white Country music and Rhythm and Blues. Southerners like Buddy Holly, Jerry Lee Lewis, and Elvis Presley fused these styles into a hybrid sound called "rockabilly." They wrote brisk and brittle songs, laced with fiery verbal cadenzas and meant to be belted across, with a whole lotta shakin' goin' on. Elvis Presley earned his first million by paring lyrics down to a throbbing series of low moans and raunchy country hollers. He helped establish the tradition of sound-as-content, which has dominated rock since it moved north and captured the cities.

By the late Fifties, Presley's wail had become the cry of the city streets. Every corner worth its traffic light had a resident group—and a surly lot they were. To uninitiated ears, theirs was punk-music: coarse, constrained, and claustrophobic. But, in fact, these superstars from the slums had democratized rock. Today's music is far too complex and the cost of instruments alone too staggering to permit mass participation. But in 1958, all the equipment a beginning group needed was a plastic pitchpipe, and all it had to master to start rocking was the five vowels.

Sha da da da
Sha da da da da,
Sha da da da
Sha da da da da,
Yip yip yip yip
Yip yip yip yip
Mum mum mum mum
Mum mum
Get a job.*

The pop song had become a chant, carried by four or five voices in a dissonant wail. Measured against the aesthetic standards of current rock, these nonsense syllables may seem ignoble. But the primary purpose of a lyric in 1957 was to convey mood, not meaning. The ideal scat song had to be simple enough for any voice to master, but intriguing enough to survive incessant repetition. Though they look absurd on paper (except, perhaps, as examples of concrete poetry), it is impossible to even read these lyrics without becoming immersed in their rhythmic pulse. That involvement was the experience these songs were intended to provide. Enshrined within the music of the late Fifties, like a sacred litany, they survive to this day, as do the unsteady bass and furious falsetto with which street singers assaulted a melody when their voices were the only instruments, and the only echo chamber within reach was under the neighborhood "el."

Without this heritage, rock is a bushel of pretty leaves pretending to be a tree. The Beatles could not have written "She Loves You" or even "I Am the Walrus" without first experiencing "Get a Job." No young lyricist works in a stylistic vacuum. Even Leonard Cohen, a recognized Canadian poet who has recently turned to song-writing, says he prepared for his new role by listening to old Ray Charles records until they warped. It shows. Cohen's rock songs have the consistency of modern verse, but unlike linear poetry, they are wrapped tightly around a rhythmic spine.

> Suzanne takes your hand
> And she leads you to the river.
> She is wearing rags and feathers
> From Salvation Army counters,
> And the sun pours down like honey
> On our lady of the harbor;
> And she shows you where to look
> Among the garbage and the flowers.
> There are heroes in the seaweed,
> There are children in the morning,
> They are leaning out for love,
> And they will lean that way forever
> While Suzanne, she holds the mirror.*

It is impossible to speak of poetry in rock without mentioning the pervasive influence of rhythm. Until recently, rigid conventions kept pop lyrics imprisoned within a metrical framework that poets had discarded long ago. Even the most adventurous lyricists wrote even stanzas, made frequent use of rhyme, and kept that mighty beat churning through their words. Today, these rules are regarded as more of a legacy than an ultimatum. But most rock creators still rely heavily on basics. Even Dylan, who comes closest to capturing the feel of modern verse in his songs, usually caps his lines with rhyme.

> Ah, get born, keep warm
> Short pants, romance, learn to dance
> Get dressed, get blessed
> Try to be a success
> Please her, please him, buy gifts
> Don't steal, don't lift
> Twenty years of schoolin'

5

And they put you on the day shift
Look out kid, they keep it all hid
Better jump down a manhole
Light yourself a candle, don't wear sandals
Try to avoid the scandals
Don't wanna be a bum
You better chew gum
The pump don't work
'Cause the vandals took the handles.*

One lesson we have learned from blues is that a familiar form can produce both great art and drivel. The crucial factor is not the style, but those who choose to work in it. Probably no one has had a greater influence on the texture of modern rock than Bob Dylan. He demolished the narrow line and lean stanzas that once dominated pop, replacing them with a more flexible organic structure. His rambling ballads killed the three-minute song and helped establish the album as a basic tool for communication in rock.

More important, he turned pop composers on to themselves. The introspective music that followed has come to black fruition in groups like the Doors. But it was Dylan's success which established beyond a doubt that poetic imagery belonged in pop music. To claim that he is the major poet of his generation is not to relegate written verse to the graveyard of cultural irrelevance. Most young people are aware of linear poetry. But they groove on Dylan, not because the rock medium has overwhelmed his message for this generation, but because, in Dylan's songs, the two reinforce each other.

This, of course, is no accident. Dylan's intention is to reconcile poetry with song. Scattered throughout his liner notes are constant references to this aesthetic task ("a song is anything that can walk by itself / i am a songwriter. a poem is a naked person . . . some people say i am a poet"). He juxtaposes symbols of high and low culture as though classicism were a haughty lady being raped by a bluesy stud. If hearing "Desolation Row" is like discovering a plastic Parthenon in a Times Square souvenir stand, that is exactly the effect Dylan means his rock-apocalypse to convey.

Praise be to Nero's Neptune
The Titanic sails at dawn
Everybody's shouting
Which side are you on?
And Ezra Pound and T. S. Eliot
Are fighting in the captain's tower
While calypso singers laugh at them
And fishermen hold flowers.*

Dylan's remarkable achievement has been to inject pop
music with poetic power by simply grafting his own sensibility onto what was already implicit in rock. As weighty
as his lyrics sometimes read, they never sound artificial on
record, because even their inconsistencies are intrinsic to
rock. For a poet who likes to speak in tongues, as Dylan often
does, pop music offers a fertile field for exploration. Rock
composers have always employed symbols (cars, roses, blue
suede shoes). Even in a classic ballad like "To Know Him
Is to Love Him," the cliches of teenage romance are used
to express something much deeper. The lyric ("I'd be good
to him / I'd bring love to him / Everyone says there'll
come a time / When I'll walk alongside of him") becomes
a chilling example of indirection when you realize that its
author, Phil Spector, took his title and refrain from the
epitaph on his father's tombstone.

Such ambiguity has existed in rock since its earliest
days, and for the most elemental reason. To sell, a pop
song had to be meaningful, but to get on the radio, it
had to sound harmless. Disc jockeys with a more rigid
sense of propriety than the most bluenosed censor actually
helped foster in young writers a profound awareness of
slang and its implications. The ability of today's lyricist
to say extraordinary things in ordinary words has its roots
in the enforced ambiguity of top-40 radio, where composers tried to express the forbidden in the context of the
permissible.

I am a back door man,
I am a back door man,
Well, the men don't know,
But the little girls understand.*

Slang is to rock what classical allusions are to written
poetry. It began as a simple code, freely adapted from

7

blues or jazz, but it soon became a major mode of communicating attitudes. Rock writers expertly hid meaning behind stray vowels and half-muttered phrases, a practice which survives to this day on some Beatle records. The penalty for failure—when sensuality became too apparent or the code too explicit—was exclusion from the radio. Just last year, an innocent-sounding ballad called "That Acapulo Gold" was yanked off the air when disc jockeys realized that its title referred to a high quality of Mexican pot.

But slang still eludes the dubious ears of disc jockeys often enough to provide a mass-snicker for the pop audiences. Today's rock poets deal with the drug experience in poeticized code, as jazzmen and blues singers before them did. It is enough for Grace Slick of the Jefferson Airplane to cry "Feed your head!" at the end of "White Rabbit" for teenagers to understand her suggestion. And John Phillips of the Mamas and the Papas has only to arch his brow over a lyric to make it seem ambiguous:

> Baby, what you're holding
> Half of that belongs to me
> 'Cause I'm a real straight shooter
> If you know what I mean.*

In a sense, this awareness of jargon is one sign of a repressed culture. But it has also provided teenagers everywhere with a solid sense of their own identity—something all good poetry is supposed to convey. So, it is almost sad to note that the golden age of rock slang is passing away. With the growth of liberal radio stations across the FM dial, lyricists are now becoming increasingly direct. Those mangy young savages from England, who could make even a virtuous love song sound like statutory rape, helped force this new frankness upon our virgin ears. With their long hair, tight pants, and eyes squinting like a dirty word, these angry musicians poured a defiant vitality into rock. Ten years ago, Chuck Berry had to content himself with indirect protest ("Don't bother me, leave me alone, / Anyway I'm almost grown"). You had to strain to catch the anger in those words, though it was present. But there's no doubt what Peter Townshend of the Who feels when he shouts:

> People try to put us down
> Just because we get around.
> Things they do look awful cold
> Hope I die before I get old.
> This is my generation, baby.
> Why don't you all f-f-f-fade away.*

With no further need for indirection in theme or language, rock poets are beginning to regard ambiguity as an enhancement rather than a necessity. For all its frankness, liberated rock remains a devious music. Lyricists still bury meanings deep within their songs. An undertone of irony is still cultivated, and sometimes lyric and melody are pitted against each other in emotional counterpoint. The BeeGees, experts at mood manipulation, often set singsong lyrics about love and devotion against tense, mournful melodies. In "Lady Jane," Mick Jagger of the Rolling Stones is a knight-errant with five days' growth of beard. He sings a chivalric ode against a tinkling dulcimer, but he keeps his voice thick, grainy, and unmistakably indelicate.

Even in their early days, the Beatles were far from tame. In the beginning their lyrics seemed as straightlaced as the collarless suits they wore then. But there was always a smirk behind those innocent shouts of "Yeah! Yeah! Yeah!" When the creators of a recent television documentary about youth culture chose to score some war footage with a Beatle ballad called "We Can Work It Out," they discovered that this gentle love song actually contained an implicit anti-war message as well ("Life is much too short for fussin' and fightin' my friend").

By 1965, the Beatles had begun to apply Dylan's freewheeling vision, and the result was a flowering of their own talent.

> I once had a girl
> Or should I say
> She once had me;
>
> She showed me her room,
> Isn't it good
> Norwegian Wood?

9

Though it doesn't look very liberated, "Norwegian Wood" is an important clue to the development of the Beatles' distinctive style. It begins easily enough, with a frank appraisal of the situation, and a concise glimpse of the hunter stalking his prey.

> I sat on a rug
> Biding my time,
> Drinking her wine.
>
> We talked until two
> And then she said
> "It's time for bed."

Using only the starkest of language, the Beatles create a tantalizing, but stubbornly non-specific scene. What goes on? Why does the narrator inform us, in a wry undertone, that he "crawled off to sleep in the bath"? And this Norwegian Wood; could that be yet another word for pot?

> And when I awoke
> I was alone,
> This bird had flown.
>
> So I built a fire,
> Isn't it good
> Norwegian Wood?*

This non-resolution was a strange twist for the lads who crooned, "I wanna hold your hand." Future Beatle songs would become even less specific, their implications even more uncertain, and when John Lennon was the author, their language more ingenious. Lennon's power as a lyricist is greatest when he rips apart the actual texture of words and re-arranges them into a sly puzzle, which is somehow as compelling as it is cryptic.

> Semolina pilchard climbing up the Eiffel Tower
> Elementary penguin, singing Hare Krishna
> Man you should have seen them kicking
> Edgar Allen POE.
> They are the eggman, I am the eggman, I am the walrus,
> Goo goo goo joob.*

From the Beatles, and from Dylan, rock poetry radiates in every direction. There is the pastel lyricism of Donovan, the literate narrative of Paul Simon, the gentle folkiness of

John Sebastian, and the raunchy power of the San Francisco blues bands. There are dozens more—all young poets who call their lyrics "pop."

But do these lyrics really amount to art? Does Wordsworth speak to Donovan from the great beyond? Is John Lennon's wordplay truly Joycean? Is Bob Dylan the Walt Whitman of the juke-box? In a sense, assertions like these are the worst enemy of liberated rock. They enslave it with an artificial heritage. The great vitality of the pop revolution has been its liberation from such encumbrances of form. Rock swings free, embracing chaos, and laughing at the notion that there could be anything more worth celebrating than the present.

Rock is, and always has been, the sacred squeal of now. It's got a damned good beat. And you can dance to it.

1.

RAUNCH AND ROOTS

How could we have faced the fifties without Chuck Berry? He helped us survive that oppressive spinach-culture, with its sexless platitudes and arthritic rhythms. Suddenly you could forget all the sugar-and-spice sterility that passed for pop. Chuck Berry was sex, speed, and see-you-later-Alligator jive. While Allen Ginsberg howled, he rocked. Remembering them both in the cultural hereafter, we will probably dig Ginsberg and dance to Berry.

The three songs which follow illustrate the range and vitality of Chuck Berry's vision. In "Mabellene" (often credited as the first rock hit) he introduced the classic car-girl ambiguity which was to haunt pop culture until the surfers resolved the confusion by treating women as just another perfect wave. "Almost Grown" set the pattern for generational protest within rock. You had to dig deep to find anger, but it was there, submerged under that playful beat.

Finally, "Rock 'n' Roll Music" presents the most important lesson pop has to offer: that energy is enough. At a time when complacency was widely equated with respectability, Chuck Berry's passionate intensity verged on the obscene. Today, when we expect to find significant poetry in rock, his lyrics seem simplistic and primitive. But it is well to remember Chuck Berry as more than a wide-eyed wailer. He was an erratic composer of unwieldy songs, but he produced an authentic rock libretto of America in the fifties. Read it and relive.

Rock 'n' Roll Music

I've got no kick against modern jazz,
Unless they try to play it too darn fast;
And change the beauty of the melody,
Until they sound just like a symphony,
That's why I go for that rock 'n' roll music
Any old way you choose it;
It's got a back beat, you can't lose it,
Any old time you use it.
It's gotta be rock 'n' roll music
If you wanna dance with me,
If you wanna dance with me.

I took my loved one over 'cross the tracks,
So she can hear my man a-wail a sax;
I must admit they have a rockin' band,
Man, they were goin' like a hurrican'
That's why I go for that rock 'n' roll music,
Any old way you choose it;
It's got a back beat, you can't lose it,
Any old time you use it;
It's gotta be rock 'n' roll music
If you wanna dance with me,
If you wanna dance with me.

'Way down South they gave a jubilee,
The jokey folks they had a jamboree;
They're drinkin' home-brew from a water cup,
The folks dancin' got all shook up.
And started playin' that rock 'n' roll music
Any old way you choose it,
It's got a back beat, you can't lose it
Any old time you use it.
It's gotta be rock 'n' roll music,
If you wanna dance with me,
If you wanna dance with me.

Don't care to hear 'em play a tango,
I'm in no mood to hear a mambo;
It's 'way too early for a congo,
So keep a-rockin' that piano.
So I can hear some of that rock 'n' roll music,
Any old way you choose it.
It's got a back beat, you can't lose it
Any old time you use it.
It's gotta be rock 'n' roll music
If you wanna dance with me,
If you wanna dance with me.

—Chuck Berry

Almost Grown

Yeah, I'm doing all right in school,
They ain't said I've broke no rule,
I ain't never been in Dutch,
I don't browse around too much;
Don't bother me, leave me alone,
Anyway I'm almost grown.

I don't run around with no mob,
I got myself a little job.
I'm gonna buy myself a little car,
I'll drive my girl in the park;
Don't bother me, leave me alone,
Anyway I'm almost grown.

I got my eye on a little girl,
Ah, she's really out of this world,
When I take her out to a dance,
She's gotta talk about romance;
Don't bother me, leave me alone,
Anyway I'm almost grown.

You know I'm still livin' in town,
But I done married and settled down,
Now I really have a ball,
So I don't browse around at all;
Don't bother me, leave me alone,
Anyway I'm almost grown.

—Chuck Berry

Mabellene

Mabellene, why can't you be true?
Oh! Mabellene, why can't you be true?
You've started back doin' the things you used to do.

As I was motivatin' over the hill,
I saw Mabellene in a Coup de Ville,
A Cadillac a-rollin' on the open road
Nothin' will outrun my V.8 Ford.
The Cadillac goin' 'bout ninety-five,
She's bumper to bumper, rollin' side by side.
Mabellene, why can't you be true?
Oh! Mabellene, why can't you be true?
You've started back doin' the things you used to do.

The Cadillac pulled up ahead of the Ford,
The Ford got hot and wouldn't do no more,
It then got cloudy and started to rain,
I tooted my horn for a passin' lane,
The rainwater blowin' all under my hood
I know that I was doin' my motor good.
Mabellene, why can't you be true?
Oh! Mabellene, why can't you be true?
You've started back doin' the things you used to do.

The motor cooled down, and heat went down
And that's when I heard that highway sound,
The Cadillac a-sittin' like a ton of lead,
A hundred and ten half a mile ahead.
The Cadillac lookin' like it's sittin' still
And I caught Mabellene at the top of the hill.
Mabellene, why can't you be true?
Oh! Mabellene, why can't you be true?
You've started back doin' the things you used to do.

—Chuck Berry, Russ
Fratto & Alan Freed

Half rock, half field holler, this lyric should be read in an even shriek, with the words slurred but their meaning utterly clear. Co-author Richard Penniman is better known as Little Richard, a titan of rhythm and blues.

Long Tall Sally

Gonna tell Aunt Mary
'Bout Uncle John,
He says he has the blues
But he has a lot of fun.

Oh baby,
Yes baby,
Woo, baby,
Havin' me some fun tonight.

Well, long tall Sally
Has a lot on the ball,
And nobody cares
If she's long and tall.

Oh baby,
Yes baby,
Woo baby,
Havin' me some fun tonight.

Gonna have some fun tonight,
Gonna have some fun tonight,
We're gonna have some fun tonight,
Well, everything will be alright.
We're gonna have some fun
Gonna have some fun tonight.

Well, I saw Uncle John
With long tall Sally
He saw Aunt Mary comin'
And he ducked back in the alley.

Oh baby,
Yes baby,
Woo baby,
Havin' me some fun tonight.

—Richard Penniman,
Enotris Johnson &
Robert A. Blackwel

This backwoods conceit was conceived by the same two Broadway-billies who would later construct the urbane slapstick of the Coasters. It is a tribute to Lieber and Stoller, Tin Pan Alley's most diversified team of rock writers, that their synthesis of city-slick and country raunch still seems honest today.

Hound Dog

You ain't nothin' but a hound dog,
Cryin' all the time.
You ain't nothin' but a hound dog,
Cryin' all the time.
Well, you ain't never caught a rabbit,
And you ain't no friend of mine.

When they said you was high classed,
Well, that was just a lie.
When they said you was high classed,
Well, that was just a lie.
You ain't never caught a rabbit,
And you ain't no friend of mine.

You ain't nothin' but a hound dog,
Cryin' all the time.
You ain't nothin' but a hound dog,
Cryin' all the time.
Well, you ain't never caught a rabbit,
And you ain't no friend of mine.

—Jerry Leiber & Mike Stoller
(for Elvis Presley)

Here is a classic rockabilly love-thump, down to its scat refrain. The tone is bright, brisk, and bracing. The imagery is geared toward action rather than reflection. Read this lyric in rhythmic gasps, pausing only to enunciate key phrases like "red blue jeans." And bear in mind that the relationship between dancing and sexuality was a crucial one for the authors of this lyric, and for their young audience as well. No wonder that association appears with such frequency in rock lyrics of the middle fifties: in those days, if you couldn't move, you couldn't love.

Be-Bop-A-Lula

Be-bop-a-lula, she's my baby.
Be-bop-a-lula, I don't mean maybe.
Be-bop-a-lula, she's my baby doll, my baby doll,
   my baby doll.

She's the gal in the red blue jeans.
She's the queen of all the teens.
She's the one that I know.
She's the one that loves me so.

She's the one that's got that beat.
She's the one with the flyin' feet.
She's the one that walks around the store.
She's the one that yells "more, more, more!"

Be-bop-a-lula, she's my baby.
Be-bop-a-lula, I don't mean maybe.
Be-bop-a-lula, she's my baby doll, my baby doll,
   my baby doll.

—Gene Vincent &
Sheriff Tex Davis

Unrequited love has always been a spur to lyric poets, but I can think of no more compelling statement of un-adorned adolescent need than this lyric. Spector (who is also immortal among rock producers) shunned the traditional conceits and cliches which were smothering pop ballads. Instead, he relied on the emotions inherent in the situation he was describing for drama. Next to the gaudy chic of the typical love song, Spector's stark, declarative tone made his lyric seem powerful and real. It still does.

To Know Him Is to Love Him

To know, know, know him
Is to love, love, love him.
Just to see him smile
Makes my life worthwhile.
To know, know, know him
Is to love, love, love him,
And I do.

I'd be good to him
And I'd bring love to him.
Everyone says there'll come a day
When I'll walk alongside of him.
Yes, yes, to know him
Is to love, love, love him,
And I do.

Why can't he see,
How blind can he be?
Someday he'll see
That he was meant for me
To know, know, know him
Is to love, love, love him,
Just to see him smile
Makes my life worthwhile.
To know, know, know him
Is to love, love, love him
And I do.

—Phil Spector
(for the Teddy Bears)

The "true love" conflict in Spector's song has always plagued white pop. But it seldom appears in Rhythm and Blues. No black composer would expend so much energy over an unattainable chick. Yet, R and B is as hung up over power and prestige as white pop is on sexuality. In "Duke of Earl," our narrator symbolically elevates himself, his girl, and his turf. He dreams of nobility, and with it, the power to control his life. We can sense all we need to know about his reality through his fantasy, and that gap is what makes this ballad so poignant.

Duke of Earl

As I walk through this world,
Nothing can stop the Duke of Earl,
And you are my girl,
And no one can hurt you,
Yes I'm gonna love you
let me hold you,
'Cause I'm the Duke of Earl.

When I hold you,
You will be the Duchess of Earl,
When I walk through my Dukedom,
The paradise we will share,
I'm gonna love you
let me hold you,
'Cause I'm the Duke of Earl.

—Earl Edwards, Eugene
Dixon & Bernice Williams
(for Gene Chandler)

Here is Tin Pan Alley's attempt to come to grips with an impending social revolution. Unfortunately it reads like someone watching Harlem from the window of a passing commuter train. As a sentimentalized glimpse of poverty, "Uptown" appealed to sympathizers, but not soul brothers.

Uptown

He gets up each mornin'
And he goes downtown,
Where everyone's his boss
And he's lost in an angry land,
He's a little man.

But then he comes Uptown
Each evening to my tenement.
Uptown where folks don't
Have to pay much rent,
And when he's there with me
He can see that he's everything.
Then he's tall,
He don't crawl,
He's a king.

Downtown he's just
One of a million guys.
He don't get no breaks
And he takes all they got to give,
'Cause he's gotta live.

But then he comes Uptown
Where he can hold his head up high,
Uptown where he knows
I'll be standin' by.
And when I take his hand,
There's no man who can put him down.
The world is sweet,
It's at his feet,   —Barry Mann & Cynthia Weil
Uptown.   (for the Crystals)

"Yakety Yak" or: How Leiber and Stoller reduce the generation gap to an unbroken, unheeded chain of commands. The greatgrandfather of "Subterranean Homesick Blues" (see p. 134).

Yakety Yak

Take out the papers and the trash,
Or you don't get no spending cash.
If you don't scrub that kitchen floor
You ain't gonna rock and roll no more.
Yakety-yak.
Don't talk back.

Just finish cleaning up your room,
Let's see the dust fly with that broom.
Get all the garbage out of sight,
Or you don't go out Friday night.
Yakety-yak.
Don't talk back.

You just put on your coat and hat,
And walk yourself to the laundromat.
And when you finish doing that,
Bring in the dog and put out the cat.
Yakety-yak.
Don't talk back.

Don't you give me no dirty looks,
Your father's hip, he knows what cooks.
Just tell your hoodlum friend outside,
You ain't got time to take a ride.
Yakety-yak.
Don't talk back.

Yakety-yak.
Yakety-yak.   —Jerry Leiber & Mike Stoller
                               (for the Coasters)

More nag-rock. But "Get a Job" is distinguished by its almost obsessive reliance on sound. Considered a classic by current scatalogists, it offers a virtual catalogue of relevant nonsense syllables. After two years of yip-yip-yipping, the rock audience considered itself blessed to hear even a single couplet in simple, unmutilated English. So, "Who Put the Bomp" must be considered as a citizen's protest. As such, it was a smash hit in its own right.

Get a Job

Sha da da da
Sha da da da da,
Sha da da da
Sha da da da da,
Sha da da da
Sha da da da da,
Sha da da da
Sha da da da da,
Yip yip yip yip
Yip yip yip yip
Mum mum mum mum
Mum mum
Get a job.
Sha da da da
Sha da da da da da.

Every mornin' about this time
She gets me out of my bed
A-cryin' "Get a job."
After breakfast, every day,
She throws the want ads right my way,
And never fails to say:

"Get a job,"
Sha da da da
Sha da da da da,
Sha da da da

Sha da da da da,
Sha da da da
Sha da da da da,
Sha da da da
Sha da da da da,
Yip yip yip yip
Yip yip yip yip
Mum mum mum mum
Mum mum
Get a job.
Sha da da da
Sha da da da da.

And when I get the paper,
I read it through and through
And my girl never fails to say
If there is any work for me,
And when I go back to the house
I hear the woman's mouth
Preachin' and a-cryin'
Tells me that I'm lyin'
'Bout a job
That I never could find.

Sha da da da
Sha da da da da,
Sha da da da
Sha da da da da,
Sha da da da
Sha da da da da,
Sha da da da
Sha da da da da,
Yip yip yip yip
Yip yip yip yip
Mum mum mum mum
Mum mum
Get a job.
Sha da da da
Sha da da da da
Uh-huh
Sha da da da
Sha da da da da,
Uh-huh. . . .

—The Silhouettes

Who Put the Bomp

I'd like to thank the guy
Who wrote the song
That made my baby fall in love
With me.

Who put the bomp
In the bomp-ba bomp-ba bomp?
Who put the ram
In the ram-a-lam a-ding-dong?
Who put the bop
In the bop sh-bop sh-bop?
Who put the dit
In the dit, dit, dit, dit-da?

Who was that man?
I'd like to shake his hand,
He made my baby fall in love
With me.
Yeah!

When my baby heard
Bomp, ba-ba-bomp, ba-bom, ba-bomp bomp,
Every word went right into her heart.
And when she heard them singing:
Ram-a-lam a-lam a-ding-dong,
She said we'd never have to part.

Each time that we're alone,
Bomp, ba-ba-bomp, ba-bom, ba-bomp-bomp,
Sets my baby's heart all aglow.
And every time we dance to:
Ram-a-lam a-lam a-lam a-ding-dong,
She always says she loves me so.

So who put the bomp
In the bomp-ba bomp-ba bomp?
Who put the ram
In the ram-a-lam a-ding-dong?
Who put the bop
In the bop sh-bop sh-bop?
Who put the dit
In the dit, dit, dit, dit-da?

Who was that man?
I'd like to shake his hand.
He made my baby fall in love
With me.
Yeah!

—Barry Mann & Gerry Goffin

You're about to encounter one of the most mystifying lyrics in rock. Its ambiguous refrain almost seems cribbed from an obscure corner of Waiting for Godot. Those who like to ponder meaning can choose between a gaggle of interpretations, including one which alleges that Sally experiences a religious epiphany, and another which asserts that the whole thing is about a lesbian affair. But it's far more meaningful to grasp the song's sensual sadness than to clutch at interpretive straws. Sally's situation is the oldest cliche in rock, but the melancholic lyricism in which her scene is set is unique. It is that quality of soft despair which attracted all the explicators in the first place.

Sally, Go 'Round the Roses

Sally, go 'round the roses.
Sally, go 'round the roses.
Sally, go 'round the roses.
Sally, go 'round the pretty roses.

The roses, they can't hurt you.
No, the roses, they can't hurt you.
The roses, they can't hurt you.
No, the roses, they can't hurt you.

Sally, doncha go, doncha go downtown.
Sally, doncha go, doncha go downtown.
The saddest thing in this whole wide world
Is to see your baby with another girl.

Sally, go 'round the roses.
Sally, go 'round the roses.
Sally, go 'round the roses.
Sally, go 'round the pretty roses.

They won't tell your secrets.
They won't tell your secrets.
They won't tell your secrets.
No, the roses won't tell your secrets.

Sally, baby, cry; let your hair hang down.
Sally, baby, cry; let your hair hang down.
Sit and cry where the roses grow,
You can sit and cry and not a soul will know.

Sally, go 'round the roses.

—Zel Sanders & Lona Stevens
(for the Jaynettes)

Elvis Presley was the Rasputin of rock. He ground country funk into the nation's consciousness by treating music as though it were motion. Even with his famous hips invisible on record, there was magic in every quiver of his voice. "Heartbreak Hotel" provided Presley with his first national hit, and served most of his fans as an introduction to rhythm and blues.

Heartbreak Hotel

Now, since my baby left me
I've found a new place to dwell,
Down at the end of Lonely Street
At Heartbreak Hotel.
I'm so lonely,
I'm so lonely,
I'm so lonely,
That I could die.

And tho' it's always crowded,
You can still find some room
For broken-hearted lovers
To cry there in the gloom
And be so lonely,
Oh, so lonely,
Oh, so lonely
They could die.

The bell hop's tears keep flowing,
The desk clerk's dressed in black.
They've been so long on Lonely Street,
They never will go back.
And they're so lonely.
Oh, they're so lonely,
They're so lonely
They pray to die.

So, if your baby leaves
And you have a tale to tell,
Just take a walk down Lonely Street
To Heartbreak Hotel,
Where you'll be so lonely,
And I'll be so lonely.
We'll be so lonely
That we could die.

—Mae Boren Axton, Tommy
Durden & Elvis Presley

Willie Dixon is an unsung hero of rock (actually he is frequently sung but seldom mentioned). Besides providing pop with some of its most enduring slang, he helped infuse rhythm and blues with a rich, earthy sense of its own tradition.

He borrowed freely from classic blues songs, updating them and making them swing. The lyrics which follow offer abundant evidence of his ability to express the forbidden within the context of the permissible. This is, of course, what rock "poetry" is all about. Its imagery is always self-amplifying. A good rock lyric contains countless "possibilities." Without Willie Dixon, these possibilities might have been severely limited.

Back Door Man

I am a back door man,
I am a back door man,
Well, the men don't know,
But the little girls understand.

When ev'rybody's tryin' to sleep,
I'm somewhere makin' my midnight creep.
In the mornin' the rooster crow,
Somethin' tells me I got to go.
I am a back door man,
I am a back door man,
Well, the men don't know,
But the little girls understand.

They take me to the doctor, shot full of holes,
Nurse try to save a soul.
Killed her for murder first degree,
Judge what tried let the man go free.
I am a back door man,
I am a back door man,
Well, the men don't know,
But the little girls understand.

Stand up, cop's wife cried, don't take him down,
Rather be dead six feet in the ground.
When you come home, you can eat pork and beans,
I eats more chicken than any man's seen.
I am a back door man,
I am a back door man,
Well, the men don't know,
But the little girls understand.

—Willie Dixon

Spoonful

It could be a spoonful of diamonds,
Could be a spoonful of gold,
Just a little spoon of your precious love
Satisfies my soul.
Men lies about it,
Some of them cries about it,
Some of them dies about it,
Ev'rything fight about a spoonful,
That spoon, that spoon, that spoonful.

It could be a spoonful of coffee,
Could be a spoonful of tea,
But a little spoon of your precious love
Is good enough for me.
Men lies about it,
Some of them cries about it,
Some of them dies about it,
Ev'rything fight about a spoonful,
That spoon, that spoon, that spoonful.

It could be a spoonful of water,
Saved from the desert sand,
But one spoon of them forty fives
Saved from another man.
Men lies about it,
Some of them cries about it,
Some of them dies about it,
Ev'rything fight about a spoonful,
That spoon, that spoon, that spoonful.

—Willie Dixon

For those who think raunchy rock is dead, here's a modern example. It is crisp, concise, and suggestive. Scrawled on subway walls and tenement halls as "Wild thing, you make my thing swing," this was not the first rock lyric to sell on the simple strength of what is almost said.

Wild Thing

Wild thing,
You make my heart sing,
You make everything groovy,
Wild thing.

Wild thing,
I think I love you.
But I wanna know for sure
Come on and hold me tight.
I love you.

Wild thing,
You make my heart sing,
You make everything groovy,
Wild thing.

Wild thing,
I think you move me,
But I wanna know for sure,
Come on and hold me tight,
You move me.

Wild thing,
You make my heart sing,
You make everything groovy,
Wild thing.

—Chip Taylor
(for the Troggs)

Here is Aretha Franklin's version of Otis Redding's most popular lyric. Redding kept his images short and specific, but Aretha breaks down all the walls in this song, and builds a few of her own. She adds a sultry vagueness, and in the process, transforms this lyric from a jocular spiel about marital rights to a curvacious sermon on sexual reciprocity.

Respect

What you want
Baby, I got it.
What you need,
You know I got it.
All I'm askin' for's
A little respect, baby,
When you come home, hey, baby,
When you get home.

I ain't gonna do you wrong
Where you goin'
Ain't gonna do you wrong
'Cause I'm a woman
All I'm askin' for's
A little respect, baby,
When you get home.

I'm about to give you
All my money,
An' all I'm askin'
In return, honey,
Is to gimme my propers, baby,
When you get home, baby,
When you come home.

Oooh, your kiss is
Sweeter than honey,
And, guess what—
Here's my money.
All I want you to do for me
Is give it to me
When you get home, yeah, baby,
Whip it to me
When you get home.

R—E—S—P—E—C—T
Find out what it means to me
R—E—S—P—E—C—T
Take care of pleasin' me.
Oh—a li'l respect
Oh—hey—a li'l respect
I get tired
. . . I keep on tryin'
You're runnin' outa fuel
An' I ain't lyin',
Respect—when y' come home . . .

—Otis Redding (as inter-
preted by Aretha Franklin)

To call this song emphatic is a bit like referring to a hydrogen bomb as "decisive." Nonetheless, the Who think highly enough of its dramatic potential to include it in nearly all their concerts. The live version usually ends in an orgy of battered instruments and frenzied feedback. Some would call such behavior destructive, and this lyric violent. But those who can see beyond the burning plastic consider "My Generation" a viable sublimation. In other words, it's a hell of a lot more useful than swiping hubcaps.

My Generation

People try to put us down
Just because we get around.
Things they do look awful cold
Hope I die before I get old.

This is my generation, baby.

Why don't you all f-f-f-fade away
Don't try and dig what we all say
I'm not trying to cause a big sensation
I'm just talking 'bout my generation.

This is my generation, baby,
My generation.

—Peter Townshend
(for the Who)

2.

BALLADS
LOUD AND SOFT

Disregard, if you will, the Beatles' reputation as agitators, and examine the body of their work. For the most part, they have always been deeply concerned with nostalgia and reminiscence. Never has that interest expressed itself more sublimely than in this simple remembrance of things past. No old-timey changes here, no antiquated slang; just a deeply felt recollection of people gone "but not forgotten." You can almost feel the lurch of brakes between these lines, as the Beatles sit down and mull things over.

In My Life

There are places I'll remember
All my life though some have changed.
Some forever not for better
Some have gone and some remain.
All these places had their moments
With lovers and friends I still recall.
Some are dead and some are living,
In my life I've loved them all.

But of all these friends and lovers,
There is no one compared with you,
And these memories lose their meaning
When I think of love as something new.
Though I know I'll never lose affection
For people and things that went before,
I know I'll often stop and think about them
In my life I'll love you more.

—John Lennon & Paul
McCartney (The Beatles)

The Supremes sing like satin. Holland, Dozier and Holland weave words across a supple loom. Together, and at their best, both teams produce a sound that is driving, but chic. That's an odd combination, and lyrics have a lot to do with its success. "Baby Love" is their finest song, both for its sleek texture and subdued tone. The lines move in even strokes, like a pendulum. You can sense the ebb and flow of feminine hips behind that gently rocking refrain. There's no random chatter in this song; just plenty of space between the syllables so the Supremes can fly away.

Baby Love

Baby love
My baby love,
I need you
Oh, how I need you
But all you do is treat me bad
Break my heart and leave me sad.
Tell me what did I do wrong
To make you stay away so long.

'Cause baby love,
My baby love
Been missing you
Miss kissing you
Instead of breaking up
Let's have some kissin' and makin' up.
Don't throw our love away
In my arms you're gonna stay.
Need you, need you
Oooh, baby love.

Baby love
My baby love
Why must we separate, my love,
All of my whole life through
Never loved no one but you.
Why d'you do me like you do.
I got this need
Need to hold you once again, my love,
Feel your warm embrace, my love
Don't throw our love away
Please don't do me this way
Not happy like I used to be
Loneliness has got the best of me.

My love,
My baby love
I need you
Oh, how I need you
Why d'you do me like you do
After I been true to you
So deep in love with you
Baby, baby, baby . . .

—Holland, Dozier & Holland
(for The Supremes)

I included this ballad largely for sentimental reasons. It's another example of longing as a motif in rock romance. Take love where you find it is the moral, and shelter it when you can.

Spanish Harlem

There is a rose in Spanish Harlem,
A red rose up in Spanish Harlem.
It is a special one;
It's never seen the sun,
It only comes out when the moon is on the run
And all the stars are gleaming.
It's growing in the street
Right up through the concrete
But soft and sweet and dreaming.

There is a rose in Spanish Harlem,
A red rose up in Spanish Harlem
With eyes as black as coal
That look down in my soul
And start a fire there and then I lose control.
I have to beg your pardon,
I'm going to pick that rose
And watch her as she grows
In my garden.

—Phil Spector & Jerry Leiber
(for Ben E. King)

Arlo Guthrie (Woody's son) comes from Brooklyn and Paul Simon was raised in Queens. Both are of the middle classes and both like to sing about freedom. But it may surprise you to notice in the lyrics that follow that there is no mention of social or political activity. Rock writers have learned that equality is not quite the same as liberty. So when they speak about being free, they generally mean free from hang-ups, from authority, and most of all from obligation. Both these songs are really about having a "free head." That kind of inner liberty is one of rock's deepest concerns.

The 59th Street Bridge Song (Feelin' Groovy)

Slow down,
You move too fast.
You got to make the morning last.
Just kickin' down the cobble stones,
Lookin' for fun and feelin' Groovy.

Hello lamppost,
What-cha knowin'
I've come to watch your flowers growin'.
Ain't-cha got no rhymes for me?
Doot'in' doo-doo, feelin' Groovy.

Got no deeds to do,
No promises to keep.
I'm dappled and drowsy and ready to sleep.
Let the morningtime drop all its petals on me.
Life, I love you.
All is Groovy.

—Paul Simon
(Simon and Garfunkel)

The Motorcycle Song

I don't want a pickle,
Just want to ride on my motorsickle,
And I don't want a tickle,
'Cause I'd rather ride on my motorsickle.
And I don't want to die,
Just want a ride on my motor-
cycle.

It was late last night the other day,
I thought I'd go up and see Ray,
So I went up and I saw Ray,
There was only one thing Ray could say, was:
I don't want a pickle,
Just want to ride on my motorsickle.
And I don't want a tickle,
'Cause I'd rather ride on my motorsickle.
And I don't want to die,
Just want a ride on my motor-
cycle.

Late last night I was on my bike,
Ran into a friend named Mike;
Ran into a friend named Mike,
Mike no longer has a bike.
I don't want a pickle,
Just want to ride on my motorsickle,
And I don't want a tickle,
'Cause I'd rather ride on my motorsickle.
And I don't want to die,
Just want a ride on my motorcy-
cle.

–Arlo Guthrie

A naive song at best, this ballad remains an effective example of basic folk-rock. Its rambling narrative and "message" are deftly encased within a lyrical shell. You can hum it or think about it. And it's certainly good enough to read at graduation, which is one of the unspoken criteria for recognizing "real" poetry.

Elusive Butterfly

You might wake up some morning,
To the sound of something moving
Past your window in the wind.
And if you're quick enough to rise,
You'll catch the fleeting glimpse
Of someone's fading shadow.

Don't be concerned, it will not harm you.
It's only me pursuing something I'm not sure of.
Across my dream, with nets of wonder,
I chase the bright elusive butterfly of love.

Out on the new horizon,
You may see the floating motion
Of a distant pair of wings.
And if the sleep has left your ears,
You might hear footsteps
Running through an open meadow.

You might have heard my footsteps
Echo softly in the distance
Through the canyons of your mind.
I might have even called your name
As I ran searching after
Something to believe in.

Don't be concerned, it will not harm you.
It's only me pursuing something I'm not sure of.
Across my dream, with nets of wonder,
I chase the bright elusive butterfly of love.

You might have seen me running
Through the long abandoned ruins
Of the dreams you left behind.
If you remember something there
That glided past you followed
Close by heavy breathing,

Don't be concerned, it will not harm you.
It's only me pursuing something I'm not sure of.
Across my dream, with nets of wonder,
I chase the bright elusive butterfly of love.

—Bob Lind

John Sebastian of the Lovin' Spoonful has provided rock with some of its most graceful ballads. "Coconut Grove" is his song of inner peace and reconciliation. There is an immense calm in his imagery, and a profound celebration of that "free head" we spoke of earlier in his simple, declarative tone. In "Coconut Grove" ease is all.

Coconut Grove

It's really true how nothing matters.
No mad, mad world, and no mad hatters.
No one's pitchin' cause there ain't no batters
In Coconut Grove.

Don't bar the door. There's no one comin'
The ocean's roar will dull the drummin'
Of any city thoughts or city ways.
The ocean's breezes cool my mind,
The salty days are hers and mine
Just to do with what we want to.

Tonight we'll find a dune that's ours
And softly she will speak the stars
Until sun-up.
It's all from havin' some one knowin'
Just which way your head is blowin',
Who's always warm like in the morning
In Coconut Grove.

It's really true how nothing matters.
No mad, mad world and no mad hatters.
No one's pitchin' cause there ain't no batters
In Coconut Grove.

—John Sebastian & Zal Yanovsky
(for The Lovin' Spoonful)

It's hard to separate the pretense from the poetry in Donovan's work. More than almost anyone in modern rock, he has been guilty of image-mongering, a trade that seems to engender its own credibility gap. He burst upon the folk-rock scene with a knapsack on his back, and for a while, it looked as if England had spawned its own mini-Dylan. He has since blossomed with a mellow opulence Dylan never presumed to capture. But he has never been able to work without a context, and too often, Donovan takes his direction from the most superficial aspects of his time. First, he embraced the psychedelic gestalt, with a brogue thick enough to smoke. He dropped that scene suddenly and gracelessly, for the greener posture of transcendental meditation. Lately, he has taken to calling himself The Author, a coronation only critics are likely to attend. While all this has little to do with the quality of his verse, it is unavoidable in evaluating the range of his activity. "Sand and Foam," his most volatile lyric, is a pungent peek through the grass darkly. It ought to be read over velveteen. Fond and fleecy sinuously erotic, this is Donovan's trip through the nether-lips of existence While there, he ought to have paid less attention to the scene, and more to the scenery.

Sand and Foam

The sun was going down
Behind a tatooed tree,
And the simple act of an oar's stroke
Put diamonds in the sea;
And all because of the phosphorus
There is quantity
As I dug you diggin' me
In Mexico.

There in the valley of Scorpio,
Beneath a cross of jade,
Smoking on the seashell pipe
The gypsies had made;
We sat and we dreamed awhile
Of smugglers bringing wine,
That crystal thought-time
In Mexico.

Sitting in the chair of bamboo,
Sipping grenadine,
Straining my eyes for
A surfacing submarine;
Kingdoms of ants
Walk across my feet
I'm shakin' in my seat
In Mexico.

Grasshoppers creaking
In the velvet jungle night,
Microscopic circles in
The fluid of my sight;
Watching the black-eyed native girl
Cut and trim the lamp,
Valentino vamp
In Mexico.

—Donovan Leitch

Tuli Kupferberg is one of the few lyricists in this collection who is also a "linear" poet in his own right. (Leonard Cohen is another.) I'm fascinated by the change rock has made in his style, how the simple expediency of melody and rhythm makes his verse less verbose, less esoteric, and more lyrical. If T. S. Eliot were a young man, would he be writing rock? I doubt it. But Dylan Thomas . . .

Morning Morning

Morning morning
Feel so lonesome in the morning
Morning morning
Morning brings me grief

Sunshine sunshine
Sunshine laughs upon my face
And the glory of the growing
Puts me in my rotting place

Evening evening
Feel so lonesome in the evening
Evening evening
Evening brings me grief

Moonshine moonshine
Moonshine drugs the hills with grace
And the secret of the shining
Seeks to break my simple face

Nighttime nighttime
Kills the blood upon my cheek
Nighttime nighttime
Does not bring me to relief

Starshine starshine
Feel so loving in the starshine
Starshine starshine
Darling kiss me as I weep

—Tuli Kupferberg
(for The Fugs)

The problem of reconciling the irregular scansion of free verse with the rigid metrical requirements of rock has long confounded ambitious pop lyricists. The Incredible String Band—two young writer-musicians from England—have devised one viable solution. By alternating emphasis and melody many times during a given piece, they turn each composition into a series of subtly evolving themes. Though the lyric which appears below conveys only one aspect of their versatility, it is apparent even here that they are folk-poets of the global village. They plunge headfirst into a dozen mystical mainstreams, and emerge fragrant with the wonder and magic that is common to them all. To read this lyric is to feel in the presence of a dozen dewy-eyed children who have been asked to construct their own cosmology.

Koeeoaddi There

the natural cards revolve
  ever changing
seeded elsewhere planted
  in the garden fair grow
  trees, grow trees

tongues of the sheer wind
  setting your foot where
  the sand is untrodden
  the ocean that only
  begins

listen a woman with a
  bulldozer built this
  house of now
carving away the mountain
  whose name is your
  childhood home
we were trying to buy it
  buy it buy it
someone was found killed
  there all bones bones
  dry bones

earth water fire and air
  met together in a
  garden fair
put in a basket bound
  with skin if you
  answer this riddle
  you'll never begin

born in a house where the
  doors shut tight
shadowy fingers on the
  curtains at night
cherry tree blossom head
  high snow

a busy main road where I .
        wasn't to go
I used to sit on the garden
        wall
say hallo to people going
        by so tall
hallo to the postman's
        stubbly skin
hallo to the baker's stubbly
        grin
mrs thompson gave me a
        bear
brigitte and some people
        lived upstairs
skating on happy valley
        pond
various ministers and guards
        stood around
the ice was nice hallo the
        invisible brethren
and there was a tent you
        played cards with the
soldiers in, don't worry we
        won't send anyone
after you they screamed

but me and licorice saw the
        last of them one
misty twisty day
across the mournful
        morning moor motoring
        away
singing ladybird ladybird
        what is your wish
your wish is not granted
        unless it's a fish
your wish is not granted
        unless it's a dish
a fish on a dish is that
        what you wish

earth water fire and air
       met together in a
       garden fair
put in a basket bound
       with skin if you
       answer this riddle
       you'll never begin

              —Robin Williamson (for
                 The Incredible String Band)

Jackson Browne is a beginning songwriter, and Brian Wilson is the mettre-en-scène of the Beach Boys. Both have in common that celestial simplicity which is unique to the music of Southern California. Jackson is terse, impatient, certain. Brian is fleecy, cosmic, eager. Jackson writes with rocky seacoasts in his head; Brian is an afternoon at Disneyland. Jackson left a blossoming career as a New York folksinger because he couldn't take the emotional weather; Brian turned down canonization as the patron saint of surfers to try for something "spiritual" instead. Jackson split from Orange County with his head intact; Brian lives in Bel Air, in a purple house, with his head gloriously shattered. Jackson is skinny; Brian is chubby. They both write that way. And both are dreamers of the true California dream.

I Am a Child in These Hills

I am a child in these hills
I am away, I am alone
I am a child in these hills
And looking for water
And looking for water.

Who will show me the river
And ask me my name
There's nobody near me to do that
I have come to these hills
I will come to the river
As I choose to be gone
From the house of my father
I am a child in these hills
I am a child in these hills.

Chased from the gates of the city
By no one who touched me
I am away, I am alone
I am a child in these hills
And looking for water
And looking for life.

Who will show me the river
And ask me my name
There's nobody near me to do that
I have come to these hills
I will come to the river
As I choose to be gone
From the house of my father
I am a child in these hills
I am a child in these hills.

—Jackson Browne

Wonderful

She belongs there
Left with her liberty,
Never known
As a non-believer,
She laughs and stays
In her wonderful . . .

She knew how
To gather the forest
When God reached softly
And moved her body,
One golden locket
Quite young and loving
Her mother and father.

Farther down
The path was a mystery,
Through the roses,
The chalk and numbers,
A boy bumped
Into her wonderful . . .

She'll return
In love with her liberty,
Never known
As a non-believer,
She'll smile and thank God
For wonderful . . .

—Brian Wilson
(for The Beach Boys)

Tim Hardin's tense but tender ballads have inspired a generation of gentle rock poets. He offers them an alternative to the traditional pop love song, in a setting that is lyrical without seeming lavish. Hardin's work has been tapped profusely by superstars in search of new commercial bait. Bobby Darin's hit version of "Carpenter" brought its author out of the underground and into the eerie light of glory by association. But no one can capture Hardin's aura of the holy victim, the "shining black sheep boy." His songs, done his way, are the essence of blues—albeit without the black.

Misty Roses

You look to me
Like misty roses,
Too soft to touch,
But too lovely
To leave alone.

If I could be
Like misty roses,
I'd love you much;
You're too lovely
To leave alone.

Flowers often cry
But too late to find,
That their beauty has been lost
With their peace of mind.

You look to me
Like love forever
Too good to last,
But too lovely
Not to try.

If I believed
In love forever,
I'd forget the past.
You're too lovely
Not to try.

—Tim Hardin

If I Were a Carpenter

If I were a carpenter
And you were a lady
Would you marry me anyway,
Would you have my baby?

If a tinker were my trade
Would you still love me?
Carrying the pots I made,
Following behind me.

Save my love through loneliness,
Save my love for sorrow.
I've given you my ownliness
Come and give me your tomorrow.

If I worked my hands in wood
Would you still love me?
Answer me, Baby, "Yes I would,
I'd put you above me."

If I were a miller
At a mill wheel grinding,
Would you miss your colored box,
Your soft shoes shining?

Save my love through loneliness
Save my love for sorrow.
I've given you my ownliness,
Come and give me your tomorrow.

—Tim Hardin

John Sebastian came of age in the Greenwich Village folk 'n' funk scene, where they played gritty blues with a thumping country edge. He called that synthesis "good time music" and made it part of every rock musician's lexicon. But there was another side to Sebastian's creative skill. With fame and finesse achieved, he began to write about things like growing up, and finding a woman. These intensely evocative ballads helped introduce a soft maturity into rock love songs. "Darling, Be Home Soon" is among the strongest of Sebastian's ballads. It is earthy without sounding coarse, and emotional without seeming sentimental.

Darling, Be Home Soon

Come and talk of all the things we did today.
Hear and laugh about our funny little ways
While we have a few minutes to breathe,
And I know that it's time you must leave.

But darling be home soon.
I couldn't bear to wait an extra minute if you dawdled.
My darling be home soon.
It's not just these few hours but I've been waiting since I
    toddled
For the great relief of having you to talk to.

Now a quarter of my life is almost past.
I think I've come to see myself at last,
And I see that the time spent confused
Was the time I spent without you
And I feel myself in bloom.

So darling be home soon
I couldn't bear to wait an extra minute if you dawdled.
It's not just these few hours but I've been waiting since I
    toddled
For the great relief of having you to talk to.

Go and beat your crazy head against the sky.
Try and see beyond the houses and your eyes
It's okay to shoot the moon.

But darling be home soon.
I couldn't bear to wait an extra minute if you dawdled.
My darling be home soon.
It's not just these few hours but I've been waiting since I
    toddled
For the great relief of having you to talk to.

               —John Sebastian
                (for The Lovin' Spoonful)

San Francisco has built its reputation on country blues, belted across with almost unbearable intensity. But the bay area rock scene also has its softer moments as is evident in this, its most haunting ballad. A sense of longing is not what you might expect from the land of cable-cars and acid, but the Jefferson Airplane were never content to merely fulfill expectations.

Comin' Back to Me

The summer had inhaled
    And held its breath too long,
The winter looked the same
    As if it never had gone,
And through an open window
    Where no curtain hung,
    I saw you,
I saw you comin' back to me.

One begins to read between
    The pages of a look
The sound of sleepy music
    And suddenly you're hooked.
    I saw you,
I saw you comin' back to me.

You came to stay and
    Live my way,
Scatter my love like
    Leaves in the wind.
You always say that
    You won't go away,
But I know what it always has been,
    It always has been.

A transparent dream
        Beneath an occasional sigh,
Most of the time
        I just let it go by.
Now I wish it hadn't begun.
        I saw you,
I saw you comin' back to me.

Strolling the hill
        Overlooking the shore
I realize I been here before,
The shadow in the mist
        Could have been anyone.
        I saw you,
I saw you comin' back to me.

Small things like reasons
        Are put in a jar,
Whatever happened to wishes
        Wished on a star,
Was it just something that
        I made up for fun?
        I saw you,
I saw you comin' back to me.

—Marty Balin
(for The Jefferson Airplane)

I see this touching account of affection in an age of non-love transposed into the final scene of an Antonioni epic about the formica masses of Southern California. As the camera pans the smog-encrusted horizon, our anti-hero explains that a bad lover is very much like a crooked drug dealer, who "burns" you by supplying bad grass; both can ruin your head.

Fade out in neon.

Everybody's Been Burned

Everybody's been burned before,
Everybody knows the pain
Anyone in this place
Can tell you to your face
Why you shouldn't try to love someone.

Everybody knows it never works,
Everybody knows, and me
I know that door
That shuts just before
You get the dream you see.

I know all well how to turn, how to run,
How to hide behind the bitter wall of blue.
But you die inside
If you choose to hide
So I guess instead, I'll love you.

—David Crosby
(for The Byrds)

Johnny Cash is Dylan without a metaphor; a dark, brooding crooner who walks a tenuous line between salvation and despair. He can galvanize an audience with his hard-luck charisma. Implicit in this declaration of eternal love is the dreadful contemplation of what might happen if the object of all that devotion should prove unworthy.

I Walk the Line

I keep a close watch on this heart of mine;
I keep my eyes wide open all the time;
I keep the end up for the tie that binds.
Because you're mine
I walk the line.

I find it very, very easy to be true.
I find myself alone when day is through.
Yes, I admit that I'm a fool for you.
Because you're mine
I walk the line.

As sure as night is dark and day is light
I keep you on my mind both day and night,
And happiness I've known proves that it's right.
Because you're mine
I walk the line.

You've got a way to keep me on your side.
You give me cause for love that I can't hide,
For you I'd even try to turn the tide.
Because you're mine
I walk the line.

—Johnny Cash

No image in rock is more persistent or more compelling than the spirit of an illusive young woman. As "Lady Jane" or "Ruby Tuesday," this elusive love-spirit second-guesses even wizened old Mick Jagger by refusing to get caught in his identity nets. All-knowing and enigmatic, she makes Leonard Cohen cry for mercy and Jim Morrison cry for more. She turns on Brian Wilson and turns away Donovan. She even tickles a Beatle's fancy, then snickers while he crawls off to sleep in the bath.

But never has she been so thoroughly, so worshipfully dissected than in this woefully inconsistent ballad. It is a miracle that the song doesn't bend under the weight of all those successive similes. But the greater miracle is that, despite its lack of poise and balance, "Sad-eyed Lady" is one of Dylan's least self-conscious songs.

For me, it is also the most moving love song in rock. Even its foibles conspire to convey the paradoxical reality of its heroine; this sad-eyed lady who can be so nonchalantly strong, and so predictably weak; so innocent, yet so corrupted. Some say Dylan wrote this song for his wife. But his inspiration hardly matters. His sad-eyed lady is everyone's girl, and everyone's girl is what the love song is all about.

Sad-Eyed Lady of the Lowlands*

With your mercury mouth in the missionary times
And your eyes like smoke and your prayers like rhymes
And your silver cross and your voice like chimes
Oh, who do they think could bury you?
With your pockets well-protected at last
And your streetcar visions which you place on the grass
And your flesh like silk and your face like glass
Who could they get to carry you?

Sad-eyed lady of the lowlands
Where the sad-eyed prophet said that no man comes
My warehouse has my Arabian drums
Should I put them by your gate
Oh sad-eyed lady, should I wait?

With your sheets like metal and your belt like lace
And your deck of cards missing the jack and the ace
And your basement clothes and your hollow face
Who among them did you think could outguess you?
With your silhouette when the sunlight dims
Into your eyes where the moonlight swims
And your matchbook songs and your gypsy hymns
Who among them could try to impress you?

Sad-eyed lady of the lowlands
Where the sad-eyed prophet said that no man comes
My warehouse has my Arabian drums
Should I put them by your gate
Oh sad-eyed lady, should I wait?

Oh, the farmers and the businessmen they all did decide
To show you where the dead angels are that they used to
    hide,
But why did they pick you to sympathize with their side
How could they ever stake you?
They wish you'd accepted the blame for the farm,
But with the sea at your feet and the phony false alarm
And with the child of a hoodlum wrapped up in your arms,
How could they ever have persuaded you?

Sad-eyed lady of the lowlands
Where the sad-eyed prophet said that no man comes
My warehouse has my Arabian drums
Should I put them by your gate
Oh sad-eyed lady, should I wait?

With your sheet metal memory of Cannery Row
And your magazine husband who one day just had to go
And your gentleness now, which you just can't help but show
Who among them do you think would employ you?
Ah, you stand with your thief; you're on his parole
With your holy medallion and your fingertips that fold
And your saint-like face and your ghost-like soul
Who among them did ever think he could destroy you?

Sad-eyed lady of the lowlands
Where the sad-eyed prophet said that no man comes
My warehouse has my Arabian drums
Should I put them by your gate
Oh sad-eyed lady, should I wait?

—Bob Dylan

* Stanza three (3) of SAD-EYED LADY OF THE LOWLANDS has been deleted at the request of the publisher.

3.

ROCK
RAMBLES

It used to be simple. There were two kinds of women in rock: the goddess and the girlfriend. The former was who you dreamed about and blamed your acne on. The latter was the groovy dancer you wanted to make it with, but they said you were too young—doo wah! Except for an occasional "lady in waiting to a virgin queen," the heroine's behavior in rock was utterly predictable. She was either unobtainably alluring or abysmally chaste. You had to settle for either true love or the agony of having gone too far. Between these poles lay no middle ground, no humanity.

But all that has changed. No longer are women mere objects of worship or desire in rock. Most put out, and few regret it. And their souls won't fit into any text on societal norms. Each of the four young ladies sketched below represents her creator's personal vision, and each has earned the right to be for real.

"Suzanne" is Leonard Cohen's maiden-teacher; half lover, half avenging angel. Van Morrison's "Brown Eyed Girl" is a creature of memory, who shares love, laughter, and the past. Jim Morrison's "Fox" is at home amid the plastic shrubbery because she herself is plastic, to the roots. And "Irene" is the casual type, more at home in a gang-bang than at a chicken fry.

Suzanne

Suzanne takes you down
To her place near the river.
You can hear the boats go by,
You can stay the night beside her,
And you know that she's half-crazy
But that's why you want to be there,
And she feeds you tea and oranges
That come all the way from China,
And just when you mean to tell her
That you have no love to give her,
Then she gets you on her wave-length
And she lets the river answer
That you've always been her lover.

And you want to travel with her,
And you want to travel blind,
And you know that she can trust you
'Cause you've touched her perfect body
With your mind.

And Jesus was a sailor
When he walked upon the water
And he spent a long time watching
From a lonely wooden tower
And when he knew for certain
That only drowning men could see him,
He said, "All men shall be sailors, then,
Until the sea shall free them,"
But he, himself, was broken
Long before the sky would open.
Forsaken, almost human,
He sank beneath your wisdom
Like a stone.

And you want to travel with him,
And you want to travel blind,
And you think you'll maybe trust him
'Cause he touched your perfect body
With his mind.

Suzanne takes your hand
And she leads you to the river.
She is wearing rags and feathers
From Salvation Army counters,
And the sun pours down like honey
On our lady of the harbor;
And she shows you where to look
Among the garbage and the flowers.
There are heroes in the seaweed,
There are children in the morning,
They are leaning out for love,
And they will lean that way forever
While Suzanne, she holds the mirror.

And you want to travel with her,
You want to travel blind,
And you're sure that she can find you
'Cause she's touched her perfect body
With her mind.

—Leonard Cohen

Brown Eyed Girl

Hey, where did we go days when the rains came,
Down in the hollow playin' a new game,
Laughing and a-running, hey, hey
Skipping and a-jumping,
In the misty morning fog
With our hearts a-thumping
And you, my brown eyed girl,
You, my brown eyed girl.

Whatever happened to Tuesday and so slow
Going down in the old mine with a transistor radio
Standing in the sunlight laughing
Hiding behind a rainbow's wall
Slipping and a-sliding
All along the water fall
With you, my brown eyed girl,
You, my brown eyed girl.

So hard to find my way, now that I'm on my own
I saw you just the other day, my, how you have grown.
Cast my memory back there, Lord,
Sometime I'm overcome thinking 'bout
Making love in the green grass
Behind the stadium
With you, my brown eyed girl,
With you, my brown eyed girl.

Do you remember when we used to sing
Sha la la la la
la la la la
la la te da
Sha la la la la
la la la la
la la te da
la te da.

—Van Morrison

"Without this heritage, Rock is a bushel of pretty leaves pretending to be a tree..."

JOHNNY
CASH

"Dylan
without
metaphor

"THE EBB AND FLOW OF FEMININE HIP"
DIANA ROSS & The Supremes

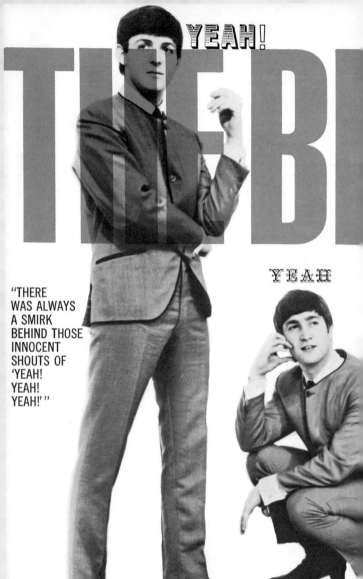

YEAH!

THE B

YEAH

"THERE WAS ALWAYS A SMIRK BEHIND THOSE INNOCENT SHOUTS OF 'YEAH! YEAH! YEAH!'"

ATLES

YEAH!

YEAH!
YEAH!
YEAH!
YEAH!

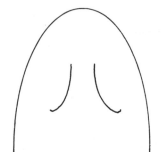

JOE TEX
"SECULAR SERMONS, FILLED WITH URBANE WIT AND STONE COUNTRY FIRE."

"THE KIND OF INNER LIBERTY THAT IS ONE
OF ROCK'S DEEPEST CONCERNS...HAVING A 'FREE HEAD'."

SIMON&GARFUNKEL

OTIS REDDING — "SWEATY, SASSY, SOUL."

PHOTO COURTESY OF ATLANTIC-ATCO RECORDS

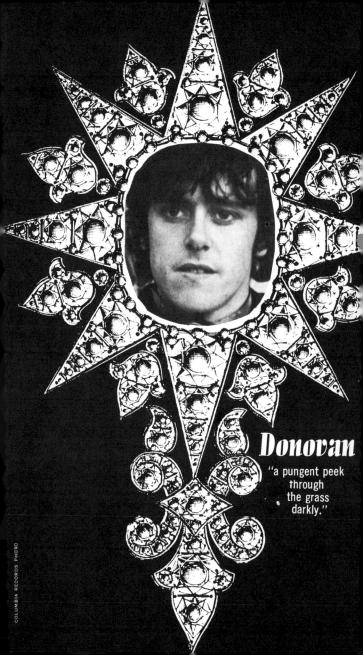

Donovan

"a pungent peek through the grass darkly."

"WHEN SHE SAYS,
'FEED YOUR HEAD!' IS SHE
REALLY ENCOURAGING
THE YOUTH OF AMERICA
TO TURN ON?
YES, IN EVERY SENSE."

GRACE SLICK
OF THE
JEFFERSON AIRPLANE

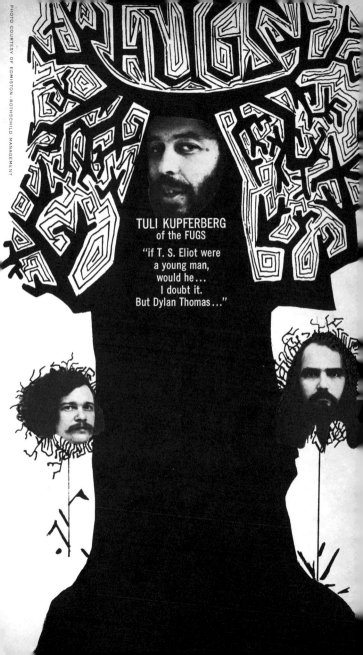

TULI KUPFERBERG
of the FUGS

"if T. S. Eliot were
a young man,
would he...
I doubt it.
But Dylan Thomas..."

John Sebastian
of the Lovin' Spoonful
'graceful ballads...gentle folkiness.'

PHOTO COURTESY OF R.J. CAVALLO MANAGEMENT, INC.

Twentieth Century Fox

Well, she's fashionably lean
And she's fashionably late.
She'll never wreck a scene,
She'll never break a date;
But she's no drag
Just watch the way she walks,
She's a twentieth century fox.

She's a twentieth century fox;
No tears, no fears,
No ruined years,
No clocks;
She's a twentieth century fox.

She's the queen of cool,
And she's the lady who waits,
Since her mind left school,
It never hesitates;
She won't waste time
On elementary talk,
She's a twentieth century fox.

She's a twentieth century fox.
Got the world
Locked up
Inside a plastic box;
She's a twentieth century fox.

—T̶̶ ̶̶ors

Motorcycle Irene

There she sits a'-smokin'
Reefer in her mouth.
Her hair hanging northward
As she travels south.
Dirty, on her Harley,
(But her nails are clean.)
Super-powered, de-flowered,
Over-eighteen Irene.

I've seen her in the bare
Where her tatoos and her chains
Wrap around her body,
Where written are the names
Of prisons she's been in,
And lovers she has seen,
Curve-winding, bumping, grinding,
Motorcycle Irene.

Ground round like hamburger
Laying in a splat
'Tis Irene, her sheen I seen
In pieces crumpled flat.
Her feet were in the bushes,
Her toes were in her hat,
Stark-ravin', un-shaven
Motorcycle Irene.

The Hunchback, the Cripple,
The Horseman, and the Fool,
Prayer books and candles, and
Carpets, cloaks, and jewels,
Knowing all the answers
Breaking all the rules,
With stark naked, unsacred,
Motorcycle Irene.

—Skip Spence
(for Moby Grape)

The new music starts here. In addition to its stunning use of ambiguity within a classic rock situation (boy meets —and fails to make—girl), this song was also the first in modern pop music to employ the sitar. The addition of what was then a bizarre musical bridge, after the line: "It's time for bed," added suspense and mystery to the song as a whole. You couldn't help looking up from your listening to wonder aloud, "What kind of guitar is that?" Then, the voices returned (ah, that reassuring nasality) only to plague you anew with a non-resolution. All this occurred at a time when the only unresolved fact about a pop song was which sound the singer made and which, he drum.

Norwegian Wood

I once had a girl,
Or should I say
She once had me;

She showed me her room,
Isn't it good
Norwegian Wood?

She asked me to stay
And she told me to sit anywhere
So I looked around
And I noticed there wasn't a chair.

I sat on a rug
Biding my time,
Drinking her wine.

We talked until two
And then she said
"It's time for bed."

She told me she worked in the morning
And started to laugh,
I told her I didn't
And crawled off to sleep in the bath.

And when I awoke
I was alone,
This bird had flown,

So I built a fire,
Isn't it good
Norwegian Wood?

—John Lennon & Paul
McCartney (The Beatles)

If she were rich, or hip, or special, she might have been the subject of a new wave film, her every twitch immortalized in cinemascope verite. But she is coarse and common and rather dull (a church goer). So, we leave her to the Beatles, who like to remind us that ordinary people also exist.

In the tradition of metaphysical poetry the Beatles invest implements of everyday existence with an overwhelming sterility. Rice, socks, cosmetics become instruments of fatalism in this song. And each stanza ends with a metaphysical question, asked in a shrug and left unanswered.

Eleanor Rigby

Ah, look at all the lonely people!
Ah, look at all the lonely people!

Eleanor Rigby
Picks up the rice in the church where a wedding has been,
Lives in a dream,
Waits at the window
Wearing the face that she keeps in a jar by the door.
Who is it for?

All the lonely people,
Where do they all come from?
All the lonely people,
Where do they all belong?

Father McKenzie,
Writing the words of a sermon that no one will hear,
No one comes near
Look at him working,
Darning his socks in the night when there's nobody there.
What does he care?

All the lonely people
Where do they all come from?
All the lonely people
Where do they all belong?

Eleanor Rigby
Died in the church and was buried along with her name.
Nobody came.
Father McKenzie,
Wiping the dirt from his hands as he walks from the grave,
No one was saved.

All the lonely people,
Where do they all come from?
All the lonely people,
Where do they all belong?

Ah, look at all the lonely people!
Ah, look at all the lonely people!

—John Lennon & Paul
McCartney (The Beatles)

For me, this is Donovan's most subtle composition, with its intricate weaving of fact and fantasy, its frank auto-erotic undertone, and its merciless exploration of ennui. It is almost as though the words were written in bleak light; that's how pale and cruel they seem.

Young Girl Blues

It's Saturday night,
It feels like a Sunday in some ways.
If you had any sense,
You'd maybe go 'way for few days.
Be that as it may,
You can only say you are lonely,
You are but a young girl
Working your way through the phonies.

Cafe on,
Milk gone.
Such a sad light
Unfading.
Yourself you'd touch
But not too much
You hear it's degrading.

The flowers on your stockings,
Wilting away in the midnight,
The book you are reading is
One man's opinion of moonlight.
Your skin is so white,
You'd like maybe to go to bed soon
Just closing your eyes,
If you were to rise up before noon.

High heels,
Car wheels.
All the losers are groovin'.
Your dream,
Straight seam,
Images are movin'.

Your friends they are making
A pop star or two every evening.
You know that scene backwards,
They can't see the pattern they're weaving.
Your friends, they're all models
But you soon got over that one.
You sit in your one room,
A little brought down in London.

Cafe on,
Milk gone,
Such a sad light
Unfading.
Yourself you'd touch
But not too much.
You hear it's degrading.

—Donovan Leitch

So much of what we define as "soul" is conveyed in performance, and so little is expressed in lyrics that the strength of modern R and B remains elusive to the naked eye. It is always the singer who socks it to you, not the song.

But Joe Tex is an exception. His lyrics are secular sermons, filled with urbane wit and stone country fire. Though no social revolutionary (he counsels fidelity and devotion), his songs remain relevant because they rarely stray beyond the province of interpersonal relationships (which usually comes down to a man and a woman). Related as a confession to an audience of witnesses, Tex's songs are the closest R and B comes to achieving a lyric significance that is profound without appearing stilted.

The Love You Save (May Be Your Own)

People I've been misled
And I've been afraid
I've been hit in the head
And left for dead.
I've been abused,
And I've been accused
Been refused a piece of bread.

But I ain't never in my life before
Seen so many love affairs go wrong
As I do today.
I want you to stop!
Find out what's wrong.
Get it right, or just leave love alone
Because the love you save today
May very well be your own.

I've been pushed around.
I've been lost and found,
I've been given 'til sundown
To get out of town.
I've been taken outside,
And I've been brutalized
And I had to be always the one to smile
And apologize.

But I ain't never in my life before
Seen so many love affairs go wrong
As I do today.
I want you to stop!
Find out what's wrong.
Get it right, or just leave love alone
Because the love you save today
May very well be your own.

—Joe Tex

Papa Was Too

Tramp!
All right baby
You can call me that,
My papa was.
'Cause I never dug workin'
From mornin' 'til night!
And the money didn't seem
To ever come out right.
(Doggone!)
Papa was a tramp,
But he was a lover too,
So why can't I
Do like papa do,
Like papa do,
Like papa do now;
'Cause I'm his son,
Why can't I be like my daddy.

Low down and nasty!
All right if you want to
Call me that, go ahead,
I guess papa was too.
Just cause I don't
Take nobody's mess,
I get mad in a minute
And jump in your chest.
Low down all right,
Papa was too,
But he was a lover.
So why can't I do,
Like my papa do,
Like papa do, like papa do;
'Cause I'm his son,
I wanna be like daddy,
I wanna be like my daddy.

Poor!
All right, call me poor, too,
'Cause papa was,
I guess he was.
Just cause I got holes
In both my shoes,
And I cover them holes
With the Daily News.
Papa was poor,
He was a lover, too.
So why can't I do,
Like my papa do
Like papa do now,
Like my papa do.
'Cause I'm his son,
Can't you understand,
I wanna be like my daddy.
I'm his son, don't you mess with me.

—Joe Tex

Roger Miller is the only contemporary country per-
former to cultivate a large rock audience as well. These
two lyrics show why. He mixes rural earthiness with
urbane whimsy and comes up with a cogent blend of
Hank Williams and Ogden Nash.

King of the Road

Trailer for sale or rent,
Rooms to let fifty cents,
No phone, no pool, no pets
I ain't got no cigarettes.
Ah, but two hours of pushing broom buys a
Eight-by-twelve four-bit room
I'm a man of means by no means
King of the Road.

Third box car midnight train
Destination Bangor, Maine,
Old worn out suit and shoes,
I don't pay no union dues.
I smoke old stogies I have found,
Short but not too big around.
I'm a man of means by no means
King of the Road.

I know every engineer on every train
All of the children and all of their names
And every handout in every town
And every lock that ain't locked when no one's around.

I sing, "Trailer for sale or rent,
Rooms to let fifty cents,"
No phone, no pool, no pets,
I ain't got no cigarettes.
Ah, but two hours of pushing broom buys a
Eight-by-twelve four-bit room
I'm a man of means by no means
King of the Road.   —Roger Miller

My Uncle Used to Love Me But She Died

My uncle used to love me but she died.
A chicken ain't chicken 'til it's lickin'-good fried.
Keep on the sunny side!
My uncle used to love me but she died.

Who'll give a quarter, thirty cents for a ring of keys;
Three sixty five for a dollar bill of groceries?
I'll have me a car of my own some day, but 'til then I
    need me a ride!
My uncle used to love me but she died.

Hamburger, cup of coffee, lettuce and tomato!
Two times a dime to see a man kiss the alligator.
One more time around free on the ferris wheel ride!
My uncle used to love me but she died!

Apples are for eating and snakes are for hissing.
I heard about hugging and I heard about kissing.
I read about it free in a fifty cent illustrated guide.
My uncle used to love me but she died!

My uncle used to love me but she died.
A chicken ain't chicken 'til it's lickin'-good fried.
Keep on the sunny side!
My uncle used to love me but she died.

—Roger Miller

Stephen Stills composed this protest anthem following a youth riot on the Sunset Strip. ("Heat" is California slang for cops . . .) It has since been regarded as a broader statement on the nature of hip resistance. Stills seems to counsel dignified passivity based on a faith in the inevitability of change. "We'll outlive them," his song seems to say. "See—we've won already."

For What It's Worth

There's something happenin' here.
What it is ain't exactly clear.
There's a man with a gun over there,
Tellin' me I've got to beware.
It's time we stop, children,
What's that sound?
Everybody look what's goin' down.

There's battle lines bein' drawn,
Nobody's right if everybody's wrong.
Young people speakin' their minds,
Gettin' so much resistance from behind.
It's time we stop, children,
What's that sound?
Everybody look what's goin' down.

What a field day for the heat.
A thousand people in the street,·
Singin' songs and carryin' signs.
Mostly saying, "Hooray for our side."
It's time we stop, children,
What's that sound?
Everybody look what's goin' down.

Paranoia strikes deep,
Into your life it will creep.
It starts when you're always afraid,
Step out of line, the Man come
And take you away.
You better stop, hey,
What's that sound?
Everybody look what's goin' down.

—Stephen Stills (for
The Buffalo Springfield)

Here is another gentle protest song. John Phillips has the most elusive head in rock. The smiling surface of his lyrics often obscures the bitterness and despair within. What a charming piece of nostalgia this lyric seems until we feel between the lines. Then we realize that warmth means love, that winter means sterility and that the preacher likes the cold.

California Dreamin'

All the leaves are brown,
And the sky is grey.
I've been for a walk
On a winter's day.
I'd be safe and warm,
If I was in L.A.
California dreamin'
On such a winter's day.

Stopped into a church
I passed along the way.
Oh, I got down on my knees
And I pretended to pray.
You know, the preacher likes the cold.
He knows I'm gonna stay.
California dreamin'
On such a winter's day.

All the leaves are brown,
And the sky is grey.
I've been for a walk
On a winter's day.
If I didn't tell her,
I could leave today.
California dreamin'
On such a winter's day.
On such a winter's day.

—John Phillips (for
The Mamas and The Papas)

To capture the heavy, humid magic of New York in heat, John Sebastian scored this lyric with atomic drumming and a real pneumatic drill. His images pound along in super-stressed bars (note the unusual emphasis on the first two syllables of nearly every verse). Sebastian isn't interested in the ease and freedom of a California summer. His is a street scene: afternoon at the pizza parlor, evening under the lamppost, then scurry to the roof for air and sex and maybe—if it's real late and everyone's asleep—privacy.

Summer in the City

Hot town,
Summer in the city.
Back o' my neck gettin' dirty and gritty.

Been down
Isn't it a pity;
Doesn't seem to be a shadow in the city.

All around
People lookin' half-dead,
Walkin' on the sidewalk hotter than a matchhead.

But at night it's a different world.
Go out and find a girl.
Come on, come on and dance all night;
Despite the heat, it'll be all right.

And babe,
Don't you know it's a pity
That the days can't be like the nights
In the summer in the city.

Cool town
Evening in the city
Dressed so fine and lookin' so pretty.

Cool cat,
Lookin' for a kitty;
Gonna look in every corner of the city.
Til I'm wheezin' like a bus stop
Running up the stairs
Gonna meet you on the rooftop.

—John Sebastian, Mark
Sebastian & Steve Boone
(for The Lovin' Spoonful)

Turning on has replaced making love as the major repository for code in rock. Like sex, drugs are usually forbidden, but often fun. Singing about drugs is a good way to get banned on the radio. But it also sells records. So you talk about getting high the way you used to mention a tumble in the tall grass—in slang. The code proliferates and bears shades of implication. Suddenly, you're not just turning on; you're partaking of something called "psychedelic culture." Suddenly, it's not just music that makes you buzz, but acid rock.

The five songs which follow are all part of the new attitude toward drugs. But they are also much more. To call these lyrics acid rock does not mean they were conceived as songs about getting high (it doesn't mean they weren't either). All that the label implies is that these lyrics were so construed by a large portion of their audience. But to take them as uniform examples of "head music" would be to miss the whole point about doing your thing in rock. If acid is a clue to the self, it must be regarded as an aesthetic neutral. What separates these lyrics from the psychedelic shlock which dominates rock is their uniquely individual approach; they are valid beyond their mythologies.

"Eight Miles High" describes a jet trip to England, but it does so in terms of a key acid-motif: the ascending airplane. "Along Comes Mary" is a compact little essay on the therapeutic value of getting high. The classic car-girl ambiguity provides a handy precedent for speaking about pot as though it were just another "rainy day woman." "Sunny Goodge Street" and "Strange Young Girls" are both scenic tours. "Goodge Street" (named for a London thoroughfare frequented by assorted freaks) contains the first explicit reference to hashish in rock ("a violent hash eater shook a chocolate machine"). But it is better remembered for its murky, mellifluous mood (". . . Mingus mellow fantastic"). John Phillips writes about acidheads on the Sunset Strip as though they were worshippers at the temple of formica ecstasy. His Fairfax freakout, set against a stately, somber melody, is in the Phillips tradition of confusing sound and meaning to mess minds.

Finally, "White Rabbit" has become a psychedelic anthem. It is Alice in Wonderland turned on, and what perfect acid rock the old fairy tale makes. Beneath its cotton candy surface lies a surreal cosmos of mysterious creatures and sinister magic. Quite a trip.

But when Grace Slick quotes the Dormouse's advice. "Feed your head," is she really encouraging the youth of America to turn on? Yes, in every sense. Rock is subversive, not because it seems to authorize sex, dope, and cheap thrills, but because it encourages its audience to make its own judgments about societal taboos. As John Phillips says in one of his lesser known lyrics: "You gotta go where you wanna go / Do what you wanna do / With whomever / You wanna do it to."

Eight Miles High

Eight miles high,
And when you touch down
You'll find that
It's stranger than known.

Signs in the street
That say where you're going
Are somewhere just
Being their own.

Nowhere is
Their warmth to be found
Among those afraid
Of losing their ground.

Rain, gray town
Known for its sound
In places
Small faces unbound.

Round the squares
Huddled in storms
Some laughing
Some just shapeless forms.

Sidewalk scenes,
And black limousines.
Some living
Some standing alone.

—Gene Clark, David Crosby &
Jim McGuinn (The Byrds)

Sunny Goodge Street

On the firefly platform on
Sunny Goodge Street,
A violent hash eater shook
A chocolate machine,
Involved in an eating scene
Smashing into neon streets in
Their stonedness
Smearing their eyes on the
Crazy colored goddess
Listening to sounds of
Mingus mellow fantastic;
"My, my," they sigh.

In doll house rooms with
Colored lights swingin'
Strange music boxes
Sadly tinklin'
Drink in the sun
Shining all around you;
"My, my," they sigh.

The magician he sparkles in
Satin and Velvet,
You gaze at his splendor with
Eyes you've not used yet,
I tell you his name is
Love, love, love.
"My, my," they sigh.
"My, my," they sigh.

—Donovan Leitch

Along Comes Mary

Everytime I think that I'm the only one who's lonely
Someone calls on me
And every now and then, I spend my time at rhyme and
     verse
And curse the faults in me
But then, along comes Mary
And does she wanna give me kicks
And be my steady chick and give me
Pick of memories?
Or maybe rather gather tales
From all the fails and tribulations
No one ever sees?

When we met
I was sure out to lunch
Now my empty cup tastes
As sweet as the punch.

When vague desire is the fire in the eyes of chicks
Whose sickness is the games they play
And when the masquerade is played and neighbor folks
Make jokes at who is most to blame today
Then along comes Mary
And does she wanna set them free
And make them see the realities in which
She got her name?
And will they struggle much when told that such
A tender touch of hers will make them
Not the same?

When we met
I was sure out to lunch
Now my empty cup tastes
As sweet as the punch.

Then when the morning of the warning's passed,
The gassed and flaccid kids are flung across the stars
The psychodramas and the traumas gone, the songs are left
     unsung
And hung upon the scars
And then along comes Mary
And does she wanna see the stains
The dead remains of all the pains
She sent the night before?
Or will their waking eyes reflect the lies
And realize their urgent cry
For sight no more?

When we met
I was sure out to lunch
Now my empty cup tastes
As sweet as the punch.

—Tandyn Almer
(for the Association)

Strange Young Girls

Strange young girls
Colored with sadness
Eyes of innocence
Hiding their madness
Walking the Strip
Sweet, soft, and placid
Offering their youth
On an altar of acid.

Thinking these kisses
Were sent by the dove
Off on a trip
Accompanied by love
Gentle young girls
Holding hands walking
Wisdom flows childlike
While softly talking.

Colors surround them
Bejewelling their hair
Visions astound them
Demanding their share
Children of Orpheus
Called by the dove
Off on a trip
Accompanied by love.

Thinking each trip
Was sent by the dove
Off on a trip
Accompanied by love.

—John Phillips (for
The Mamas and The Papas)

White Rabbit

One pill makes you larger
And one pill makes you small.
And the ones that mother gives you
Don't do anything at all.
Go ask Alice
When she's ten feet tall.

And if you go chasing rabbits
And you know you're going to fall.
Tell 'em a hookah smoking caterpillar
Has given you the call.
Call Alice
When she was just small.

When men on the chessboard
Get up and tell you where to go.
And you've just had some kind of mushroom
And your mind is moving low.
Go ask Alice
I think she'll know.

When logic and proportion
Have fallen sloppy dead,
And the White Knight is talking backwards
And the Red Queen's lost her head

Remember what the dormouse said:
"Feed your head.
Feed your head.
Feed your head."

—Grace Slick
(of The Jefferson Airplane)

4.

ALLEGORY AND BEYOND

Interpreting Dylan is a dangerous occupation; I liken it to running a U.S.O. in Hanoi. The chances of being hit by flak are staggering. So I won't try to define "Desolation Row." Any attempt to ground Dylan's open-ended imagery seems to shed more light on the interpreter's concept of reality than on the song itself. The best way to understand Dylan and his lyric poetry is to follow the scenes he sets, and the roles his characters pretend to play. And bear in mind, when pressed for particulars, that William Burroughs writing a Divine Comedy in drag might well set it on a thoroughfare like Desolation Row.

Desolation Row*

They're selling postcards of the hanging
They're painting the passports brown
The beauty parlor's filled with sailors
The circus is in town
Here comes the blind commissioner
They've got him in a trance
One hand's tied to the tight-rope walker
The other is in his pants
And the riot squad they're restless
They need somewhere to go
As lady and I look out tonight
From Desolation row

Cinderella she seems so easy
It takes one to know one she smiles
Then puts her hands in her back pocket
Bette Davis style
Then in comes Romeo he's moaning
You belong to me I believe
Then someone says you're in the wrong place my friend
You'd better leave
And the only sound that's left
After the ambulances go
Is Cinderella sweeping up
On Desolation Row.

Now the moon is almost hidden
The stars are beginning to hide
The fortune telling lady
Has even taken all her things inside
All except for Cain and Abel
And the hunchback of Notre Dame
Everybody is making love
Or else expecting rain
And the good samaritan he's dressing
He's getting ready for the show
He's going to the carnival
Tonight on Desolation Row.

Einstein disguised as Robin Hood
With his memories in a trunk
Passed this way an hour ago
With his friend a jealous monk
He looked so immaculately frightful
As he bummed a cigarette
Then he went off sniffing drain pipes
And reciting the alphabet
Now you would not think to look at him
But he was famous long ago
For playing the electric violin
On Desolation Row.

Doctor filth he keeps his word
Inside of a leather cup
But all his sexless patients
They're trying to blow it up
Now his nurse some local loser
She's in charge of the cyanide hold
And she also keeps the cards that read
Have mercy on his soul
They all play on penny whistles
You can hear them blow
If you lean your head out far enough
From Desolation Row.

Across the street they've nailed the curtains
They're getting ready for the feast
The phantom of the opera
A perfect image of a priest
They're spoon feeding Casanova
To get him to feel more assured
Then they'll kill him with self confidence
After poisoning him with words
And the phantom shouting to skinny girls
Get outta here if you don't know
Casanova is just being punished
For going to Desolation Row.

Now at midnight all the agents
And the super human crew
Come out and round up everyone
That knows more than they do
Then they bring them to the factory
Where the heart attack machine
Is strapped across their shoulders
And then the kerosene
Is brought down from the castles
By insurance men who go
Check to see that nobody is escaping
To Desolation Row.

Praise be to Nero's Neptune
The Titanic sails at dawn
Everybody's shouting
Which side are you on?
And Ezra Pound and T. S. Eliot
Are fighting in the captain's tower
While calypso singers laugh at them
And fishermen hold flowers
Between the windows of the sea
Where lovely mermaids flow
And nobody has to think too much
About Desolation Row.

Here is Peter Townshend's vision of psychic plasticity
American audiences were deemed mature (or thick
headed) enough to accept its incestual implications, but
not its racial ones. The line about our hero's mixed origin
was deleted.

Substitute

You think we look pretty good together.
You think my shoes are made of leather.
But I'm a substitute for another guy.
I look pretty tall but my heels are high.
The simple things you see are all complicated.
I look pretty young but I'm just back dated.
Yeah!

It's a substitute lies for fact.
I can see right through your plastic mac.
I look all white but my dad was black.
My fine-looking suit is really made out of sack.

I was born with a plastic spoon in my mouth.
Northside of my town faces East and the Eastside faces
    South.
And now you dare to look me in the eye.
But crocodile tears are what you cry.
If it's a genuine problem you won't try
To work it out at all, just pass it by.
Pass it by!

Substitute me for him.
Substitute like coke for gin.
I substitute you for my mum.
At least I get my washing done.

—Peter Townshend
(for The Who)

In her best lyric, Janis Ian manages to transcend the parental conflict which absorbs so much of her creative energy. Yet, even her Christ figure is martyred by authority, condemned by both his hip peers and a parental Pilate, who stands offstage, scrubbing up for the kill.

New Christ Cardiac Hero

Yesterday's preacher, today's bikini beacher,
They've stolen your clerical robes and your Bible's been thrown.
Your virgin red crown of thorns has turned to ivory horns
And your corner throne it has become a coroner's stone.
The crucifix you prayed on turned to jailhouse bars;
Its silver chain you left out in the rain to glow with dust
And turned to seaweed tangled in your heart.
Now how does it feel to pull out the nails and find you still can walk?
Oh, you can't feel at all from your self-imposed rack on the wall.
The tighter you drive the nails, oh, the harder you'll fall.
So come on down, come off it, Sir, you're gonna get hurt.

The holy water you bathe in mingles with the sewer,
All your disciples have reclaimed their rifles and taken the cure.
Your lectures of ways are only today's poolroom jokes
Scrawled on the walls of tenement halls and bathroom bowls.
As jingle bells cry pay us well or you'll go to hell.
Freedom's chains bind your pain and tie you well,
But how could you know the gallows you hold weighs you down?
Now isn't it boss, you don't need a cross to get around.

The eyes that cried for mankind's pride are covered with
    shades
As the children of God trample unshod past your mindly
    grave.
And the new Christ hipster cardiac hero of 2,000 years
    past your mind
Spits at your feet, crying "We have no need of God, each
    of us is his own."
Yesterday's preacher, today's bikini beacher,
They've stolen your clerical robes, your Bible's been thrown
You must have a cross, but they've taken you, God, and
    shot you filled with dead,
So following new Christ pick up on a cycle instead.

                                    —Janis Ian

Penny Lane

Penny Lane: There is a barber taking photographs
Of every head he's had the pleasure to know.
And all the people that come and go
Stop and say hello.

On the corner is a banker with a motor car.
The little children laugh at him behind his back.
And the banker never wears a mac
In the pouring rain,
Very strange!

Penny Lane is in my ears and in my eyes,
Wet beneath the blue suburban skies,
I sit and meanwhile, back in Penny Lane:
There is a fireman with an hour glass
And in his pocket is a portrait of the queen,
He likes to keep his fire engine clean,
It's a clean machine.

Penny Lane is in my ears and in my eyes,
Full of fish-and-finger pies
In summer, meanwhile, back behind the
Shelter in the middle of the round-a-bout
A pretty nurse is selling poppies from a tray,
And tho' she feels as if she's in a play
She is anyway.

Penny Lane: The barber shaves another customer
We see the banker sitting, waiting for a trend.
And then the fireman rushes in
From the pouring rain,
Very strange!

Penny Lane is in my ears and in my eyes,
Wet beneath the blue suburban skies.

—John Lennon & Paul
McCartney (The Beatles)

Procol Harum is only a rock group. Yet it shook the pop world with the two epic ditties which appear below. They were the biggest hits since "Winchester Cathedral" (so much for precedent). Stripped of their rhythmic robes, these lyrics make ponderous poetry. In fact, they reek of random allusions and post-graduate funk.

But fortunately they weren't meant to drive Robert Lowell into retirement. As mere songs, they have an uncanny power to stand above their pretensions and seem unique, if not authentic. "Homburg" is the better lyric, I think. Far below its cerebral frosting you can sense an undertone of stark, bitter sensuality.

Procol Harum reminds me of an intellectual, ever fighting to suppress his Steppenwolf, and never realizing that the beast within is all that makes him tolerable.

A Whiter Shade of Pale

We skipped the light fandango
And turned cartwheels cross the floor.
I was feeling kind of seasick
But the crowd called out for more.
The room was humming harder
As the ceiling flew away
When we called out for another drink
The waiter brought a tray
And so it was that later
As the miller told his tale
That her face at first just ghostly
Turned a whiter shade of pale.

She said "There is no reason,
And the truth is plain to see,"
But I wandered through my playing cards
And would not let her be
One of sixteen vestal virgins
Who were leaving for the coast
And although my eyes were open
They might just have well been closed.
And so it was that later
As the miller told his tale
That her face at first just ghostly
Turned a whiter shade of pale.

—Keith Reid & Gary Brooker
(for Procol Harum)

Homburg

Your multilingual business friend
Has packed her bags and fled
Leaving only ashfilled ashtrays
And the lipsticked, unmade bed.
The mirror on reflection
Has climbed back upon the wall
For the floor she found descended
And the ceiling was too tall.

Your trouser cuffs are dirty
Your shoes are laced up wrong
You'd better take off your homburg
'Cause your overcoat is too long.

The town clock in the market square
Stands waiting for the hour
When its hands, they both turn backwards,
And on meeting will devour
Both themselves and also any fool
Who dares to tell the time
And sun and moon will shudder
And the signposts cease to sign.

Your trouser cuffs are dirty
Your shoes are laced up wrong
You'd better take off your homburg
'Cause your overcoat is too long.

—Keith Reid
(for Procol Harum)

Here is Leonard Cohen's "beautiful loser," in verse. You love this hung-up saint with his three day beard and running nose of the soul. You want to take him home, feed him chicken soup, and worship his suffering. Sure he's down—gloriously down—but you know he can make it up again.

So does he!

Dress Rehearsal Rag

Got up some time in the afternoon
And you didn't feel like much.
Said to yourself, 'Where are you, Golden Boy
Where is your famous golden touch?
I thought you knew where all the elephants lie down
I thought you were the crown prince of all the wheels in
    Ivory town.'
Look at your body now
Well, there's nothing much to save
And the bitter voice in the mirror says,
'Hey, Prince, you need a shave.'
That's right, it's come to this
It's come to this
And wasn't it a long way down?
And wasn't it a strange way down?

There's no hot water
And the cold is running thin
Well, what do you expect from the kind of places
You've been living in?
Don't drink from that cup,
It's all caked and cracked along the rim.
That's not the electric light, my friend,
That's your vision that is dim.
Cover up your face with soap,
There—now you're Santa Claus
And you've got an A for anyone

Who will give you his applause.
I thought you were a racing man
Ah, but you couldn't take the pace
There's a funeral in the mirror
And it's stopping at your face
That's right—it's come to this
It's come to this
And wasn't it a long way down?
And wasn't it a strange way down?

Once there was a path
And a girl with chestnut hair
And you spent the summers picking
All the berries that grew there
There were times she was a woman
There were times she was a child
As you held her in the shadows
Where the raspberries grew wild
And you climbed the highest mountains
And you sang about the view
And everywhere you went
Love went along with you
That's a hard one to remember
It makes you clench your fist.
And the veins stand out like highways
All along your wrist
And yes, it's come to this
It's come to this
And wasn't it a long way down?
And wasn't it a strange way down?

You can still find a job
Go out and talk to a friend
On the back of every magazine
There are coupons you can send
Why don't you join the Rosicrucians?
They will give you back your hope.
You can find your love in diagrams
In a plain brown envelope
But you've used up all your coupons
Except the one that seems

To be tatooed on your arm
Along with several thousand dreams
Now Santa Claus comes forward
That razor in his mitt
And he puts on his dark glasses
And he shows you where to hit
And then the cameras pan
The stand-in stunt man's
Dress Rehearsal Rag.

—Leonard Cohen

Of all the lyrics in this book, "A Day in the Life" has had the most immediately profound effect on its audience. It was received as an immortal rock-poem, and it has exerted a seminal influence on rock lyrics since. It took years for Dylan's poetic sensibility to become accessible to a mass audience. But the Beatles needed no emissaries for their verse; because they drew on a tone and texture which was already established within contemporary verse, they made it easy for their audience to accept their lyrics as "poetic," and therefore, powerful.

This is not to say that "A Day in the Life" is unimaginative or stale, but its immortality is currently assured for the wrong reasons. As a poetic statement of contemporary despair, the lyric leans heavily (and intentionally) upon traditional modes. The deadened crowds, the clutch and kitsch of pop culture, and the vision of a non-hero overwhelmed by non-demands—all these images owe their lineage to T. S. Eliot and his peers. If "A Day in the Life" were merely the sum of its imagery, it would have amounted to aesthetic assimilation at its lowest (i.e., the presentation of esoteric concepts in simplified form). But the Beatles were after more than poeticized "effect" here, and the restatement of accepted poetic ideas in that neat concise verse pattern which marks their style is only the surface of this song.

What is special about "A Day in the Life" lies beneath. Music, in rock, often amplifies and elevates a meaningless lyric. Many pop lyricists find themselves faced with an ensuing problem of internal competition within their songs. If the lyric is esoteric, and the music is stunning as well, both will work against each other, and the result will be a non-poem, within a non-song. For many writers, the solution has been to keep the lyric safely subservient to the music. In employing established poetic concepts here, the Beatles alert us to "stay tuned for meaning" without destroying the force of their music. And the thrust of "A Day in the Life" is magnified through the most incredible orchestral barrage ever to grace a pop composition. There are shiftless rhythms, assaulting chords, and an unbearable crescendo (performed by full orchestra) followed by soft, sonic hum.

The entire composition revolves around an understated refrain ("I'd love to turn you on") which brims with implicit tension. But what are we to make of that line? Is it a credible statement of contemporary ennui, a reflection of psychic desperation, or the promise of a solution? The singer's voice, which is near to cracking throughout the song, becomes calm and certain whenever he sings that refrain. Is this the certainty of euphoria found, or extinction glimpsed?

A Day in the Life

I read the news today, oh boy,
About a lucky man who made the grade
And though the news was rather sad
Well I just had to laugh
I saw the photograph.
He blew his mind out in a car
He didn't notice that the lights had changed
A crowd of people stood and stared
They'd seen his face before
Nobody was really sure
If he was from the House of Lords.

I saw a film today, oh boy,
The English army had just won the war
A crowd of people turned away
But I just had to look
Having read the book.
I'd love to turn you on.

Woke up, fell out of bed,
Dragged a comb across my head
Found my way downstairs and drank a cup,
And looking up I noticed I was late.
Found my coat and grabbed my hat
Made the bus in seconds flat
Found my way upstairs and had a smoke,
Somebody spoke and I went into a dream.

I read the news today, oh boy,
Four thousand holes in Blackburn,
Lancashire
And though the holes were rather small
They had to count them all
Now they know how many holes it takes to fill the Albert
   Hall.
I'd love to turn you on.

—John Lennon & Paul
McCartney (The Beatles)

The generation gap as vaudeville: Dylan stands stage left, in Beatle cap and bluejeans brimming over with cryptic revelation. He does a mock-shuffle about parental righteousness, then stands there digging his own sense of the absurd. Warped cliches and plastic platitudes bounce off the balcony. The popcorn lady lowers the curtain and we all applaud. Dylan emerges from the wings to do his encore ("Twenty years of schoolin' and they put you on the day shift"). When it's over, we have only to wonder whether we've been watching a mimic or a prophet.

Subterranean Homesick Blues*

Johnny's in the basement
Mixing up the medicine
I'm on the pavement
Thinking about the government
The man in the trenchcoat
Badge out, laid off
Says he's got a bad cough
Wants to get paid off
Look out kid
It's something you did
God knows when
But you're doin' it again
You better duck down the alley way
Lookin' for a new friend
The man in the coonskin cap
By the big pen
Wants eleven dollar bills
You only got ten.

Get sick get well
Hang around an ink well
Ring bell, hard to tell
If anything is goin' to sell
Try hard, bet barred

Get back, write braille
Get jailed, jump bail
Join the army, if you fail
Look out kid, you're gonna get hit
But users, cheaters
Six time losers
Hang around the theatres
Girl by the whirl pool
Lookin' for a new fool
Don't follow leaders
Watch the parkin' meters.

Ah, get born, keep warm
Short pants, romance, learn to dance
Get dressed, get blessed
Try to be a success
Please her, please him, buy gifts
Don't steal, don't lift
Twenty years of schoolin'
And they put you on the day shift
Look out kid, they keep it all hid
Better jump down a manhole
Light yourself a candle, don't wear sandals
Try to avoid the scandals
Don't wanna be a bum
You better chew gum
The pump don't work
'Cause the vandals took the handles.

—Bob Dylan

Infuriating in its insistence on expressing everything in allegorical terms, this is nonetheless an important lyric since it represents a metamorphosis of the "occasional" folk ballad into poetic verse. There is a direct link between those rambling breakdowns about the assassination of McKinley and "Crucifixion," which uses John F. Kennedy's murder as a prism to explore the mythic hero in our day and our demand for his sacrifice.

Crucifixion

And the night comes again to the circle-studded sky,
The stars settle slowly, in loneliness they lie.
Till the universe explodes as a falling star is raised;
The planets are paralyzed, the mountains are amazed;
But they all glow brighter from the brilliance of the blaze;
With the speed of insanity, then, he dies!

In the green fields of turning, a baby is born;
His cries crease the wind, and mingle with the morn;
An assault upon the order, the changing of the guard;
Chosen for a challenge that's hopelessly hard;
And the only single sign is the sighing of the stars;
But to the silence of distance they're sworn!

So dance, dance, dance
Teach us to be true;
Come dance, dance, dance;
'Cause we love you.

Images of innocence charge him to go on
But the decadence of history is looking for a pawn
To a nightmare of knowledge he opens up the gate
A blinding revelation is served upon his plate
That beneath the greatest love is a hurricane of hate
And God help the critic of the dawn.

So he stands on the sea and he shouts to the shore
But the louder that he screams the longer he's ignored

For the wine of oblivion is drunk to the dregs
And the merchants of the masses almost have to be begged
Till the giant is aware that someone's pulling at his leg
And someone is tapping at the door.

So dance, dance, dance
Teach us to be true;
Come dance, dance, dance;
'Cause we love you.

Then his message gathers meaning and it spreads across
    the land
The rewarding of the fame is the following of the man
But ignorance is everywhere and people have their way
And success is an enemy to the losers of the day
In the shadows of the churches who knows what they pray
And blood is the language of the band.

The Spanish bulls are beaten, the crowd is soon beguiled
The matador is beautiful, a symphony of style
Excitement is ecstatic, passion places bets,
Gracefully he bows to ovations that he gets
But the hands that are applauding are slippery with sweat
And saliva is falling from their smiles.

So dance, dance, dance
Teach us to be true;
Come dance, dance, dance;
'Cause we love you.

Then this overflow of life is crushed into a liar
The gentle soul is ripped apart and tossed in to the fire
It's the burial of beauty, it's the victory of night.
Truth becomes a tragedy limping from the light
The heavens are horrified, they stagger from the sight
And the cross is trembling with desire.

They say they can't believe it, it's a sacrilegious shame
Now who would want to hurt such a hero of the game
But you know I predicted it I knew he had to fall
How did it happen, I hope his suffering was small
Tell me every detail I've got to know it all
And do you have a picture of the pain.

So dance, dance, dance
Teach us to be true;
Come dance, dance, dance;
'Cause we love you.

Time takes her toll and the memory fades
But his glory is growing in the magic that he made
Reality is ruined there is nothing more to fear
The drama is distorted to what they want to hear
Swimming in their sorrow in the twisting of a tear
As they wait for the new thrill parade.

The eyes of the rebel have been branded by the blind
To the safety of sterility the threat has been refined
The child was created to the slaughter house he's led
So good to be alive when the eulogies are read
The climax of emotion the worship of the dead
As the cycle of sacrifice unwinds.

So dance, dance, dance
Teach us to be true;
Come dance, dance, dance;
'Cause we love you.

And the night comes again to the circle-studded sky,
The stars settle slowly, in loneliness they lie.
Till the universe explodes as a falling star is raised;
The planets are paralyzed, the mountains are amazed;
But they all glow brighter from the brilliance of the blaze;
With the speed of insanity, then, he dies!

—Phil Ochs

Here is the BeeGees' vision of hell in little boxes. The true disaster here is one of separation between the speaker and his own existence. It is his tone of resignation—his uncanny calm—which gives this lyric its dreamlike quality. Cautiously, almost politely, he asks an apocryphal Mr. Jones about his wife. "Don't go talking too loud, you'll cause a landslide," he remarks, and we begin to wonder just how external this man's prison is. After all, there never was a New York mining disaster in 1941. Rather, the sense of inner peril which this song conveys seems to parallel Thoreau's epitaph for an age in which "the mass of men live lives of quiet desperation."

New York Mining Disaster—1941

In the event of something happening to me,
There is something I would like you all to see.
It's just a photograph of someone that I knew.

Have you seen my wife, Mister Jones?
Do you know what it's like on the outside?
Don't go talking too loud,
You'll cause a landslide, Mister Jones.

I keep straining my ears to hear a sound,
Maybe someone is digging underground.
Or have they given up and all gone home to bed
Thinking those who once existed must be dead.

Have you seen my wife, Mister Jones?
Do you know what it's like on the outside?
Don't go talking too loud,
You'll cause a landslide, Mister Jones.

—Barry & Robin Gibb
(for The BeeGees)

This is one of the earliest folk-rock statements of man's alienation from you-know-whom. Some say Paul Simon took his theme from Steppenwolf. If not, it is certainly an analogous situation and one which has provided abundant source material for rock poets. But never has it been expressed so succinctly and with such compassion.

The Sound of Silence

Hello darkness my old friend,
I've come to talk with you again,
Because a vision softly creeping,
Left its seeds while I was sleeping
And the vision that was planted in my brain
Still remains within the sound of silence.

In restless dreams I walked alone,
Narrow streets of cobble stone
'Neath the halo of a street lamp,
I turned my collar to the cold and damp
When my eyes were stabbed by the flash of a neon light
That split the night, and touched the sound of silence.

And in the naked light I saw
Ten thousand people maybe more,
People talking without speaking,
People hearing without listening,
People writing songs that voices never share
And no one dares disturb the sound of silence.

"Fools!" said I, "You do not know
Silence like a cancer grows.
Hear my words that I might teach you
Take my arms that I might reach you."
But my words like silent raindrops fell
And echoed, in the wells of silence.

And the people bowed and prayed
To the neon God they made,

And the sign flashed out its warning
In the words that it was forming.
And the sign said:
    "The words of the prophets are written
        on the subway walls and tenement halls"
And whispered in the sounds of silence.

                        —Paul Simon
                        (Simon and Garfunkel)

When Spanish galleons bound for the New World became trapped in the doldrums, they were forced to lighten their cargo—which usually consisted of horses. Struck by the "mute nostril agony" of that moment when horses hit the water, Jim Morrison wrote this haunting poem. Its words are declaimed in an even shriek until they are drowned in feedback.

Horse Latitudes

When the still sea conspires an armor
And her sullen and aborted
Currents breed tiny monsters,
True sailing is dead.

Awkward instant
And the first animal is jettisoned,
Legs furiously pumping
Their stiff green gallop,
And heads bob up
Poise
Delicate
Pause
Consent
In mute nostril agony
Carefully refined
And sealed over.

—The Doors

Contagious magic is alive and well wherever Jim Morrison and The Doors appear. Morrison himself looks every inch the street punk gone to heaven and reincarnated as a choir boy. His lyrics—amplified by the relentless rhythms of his fellow Doors—become a mighty myth of catharsis, with an Oedipal backbeat. "Break loose" is his most frequent command, and its mere utterance sends waves of sheer rapport through an audience. "The End" bristles with that exhortation. "Divine is Free," it ordains. That is an equation we are anxious to accept, rendering holy what is simply unrestrained.

The End

This is the end,
Beautiful friend,
This is the end,
My only friend,
The end of our elaborate plans,
The end of everything that stands,
The end. No safety or surprise,
The end. I'll never look into your eyes
Again.

Can you picture what will be,
So limitless and free,
Desperately in need of some stranger's hand
In a desperate land.
Lost in a Roman wilderness of pain
And all the children are insane
All the children are insane;
Waiting for the summer rain.

There's danger on the edge of town,
Ride the king's highway.
Weird scenes inside the gold mine;
Ride the king's highway west, baby.
Ride the snake
To the lake

The ancient lake.
The snake is long
Seven miles;
Ride the snake,
He's old and his skin is cold.

The West is the best.
The West is the best.
Get here and we'll do the rest.
The blue bus is calling us.
Driver, where you taking us?

The killer awoke before dawn,
He put his boots on,
He took a face from the ancient gallery,
And he walked on down the hall.
He went to the room where his sister lived,
And then he paid a visit to his brother,
And then he walked on down the hall.
And he came to a door.
And he looked inside

"Father?"
"Yes, son?"
"I want to kill you."
"Mother, I want to . . ."

Come on baby, take a chance with us,
And meet me by the back of the blue bus.

This is the end,
Beautiful friend.
This is the end,
My only friend, the end.
It hurts to set you free
But you'll never follow me
The end of laughter and soft lies,
The end of night we tried to die.
This is the end.

—The Doors

INDEX

Bantam Book Catalog

It lists over a thousand money-saving best-sellers originally priced from $3.75 to $15.00 —bestsellers that are yours now for as little as 60¢ to $2.95!

The catalog gives you a great opportunity to build your own private library at huge savings!

So don't delay any longer—send us your name and address and 25¢ (to help defray postage and handling costs).